My Observations of, and Experiences with Leadership in Management

My Observations of, and Experiences with Leadership in Management

Plus

Thoughts Expressed By
Experienced Leaders

John Stearns

To order additional copies of this book, contact:
Xlibris Corporation
1-888-795-4274
www.Xlibris.com
Orders@Xlibris.com
76461

OUTLINE—CONTENTS

To my wonderful wife of 71 years, Marguerite,
Our sons, Robert and William,
And in memory of our son, John, Jr (deceased)

For their patience, understanding,
encouragement, and support

Thoughts expressed by experienced leaders include those by-

Ray Valeika, retired from Delta Airlines as Senior Vice President, Technical Operations. Now airline consultant.

General Colin Powell, USA (retired)—

Angelo Noa—Director of the Office of Fleet Administration, NYC (retired)

Karen Rightmire - President United Way, Berks County, PA (retired)

Ralph Scott—Division Manager, ATT & T Co., (retired)

I wish to thank my former co-workers at Pan Am, Ray Valeika and Angelo Noa, for sharing their backgrounds and experiences ; my friend, Karen Rightmire, for sharing her frank opinions; my sons, Bob and Bill, for offering advice and experiences; and my new friend of recent years at Edgewater Retirement Community, Ralph Scott, for sharing his experience with supervisory training. I also thank another fellow resident of Edgewater, Henrietta Isler, Ph,D for her advice and encouragement in the publishing process. I thank the Executive Director, Edgewater Point Estates, for his encouraging comments on the first draft.

INTRODUCTION

All of my life, I have wondered why some people are leaders and others are not.

This book is sort of an analysis of the relationship between employee, supervisor, manager and leader.

In the 1970's, I had the pleasure of working out of a Pan Am training department office at JFK airport, NY, with a fellow who I "observed" as having qualities of leadership. I often thought had he been an officer in the trenches, and called "let's go", his men, without hesitation, would follow him "over the top". He was in management at Pan Am as a Maintenance Technical Instructor. I was conducting classes in management development.

Of course, he wasn't a CEO or Vice President, probably because he did not have the necessary formal education, but to me he represented the qualities I would hope to find in those positions. He planned his work, set goals and clearly communicated them to individuals or groups. He comfortably reflected a style of knowledgeable, but modest, self confidence. With a pleasant personality, he seemed to earn the trust of others. It was always evident he had prepared himself through experience and study of the subject he was teaching.

I don't know why, but to me, as I saw him perform his work, he was the natural "leader" type. Even though there were several other well qualified instructors in the group, this instructor, John Romaine, came to mind as I prepared to write this book on the subject of leadership in management.

I am aware of the many books, courses, and other materials on the subject of management, and I have read many of them, but I believe in using my personal experiences and observations, with the experience of others, it will make clear the difference between "managers" and those who are "leaders in management".

It is not my intention to write this as a "personal career" story and therefore, references to my personal experiences are only to be considered as they relate to the subject and not necessarily in chronological order.

In writing this book I am motivated by three thoughts—

First—most of my life I have mentally noted the differences in styles, manners, and methods of peoples' relationships with others. And then I found that in my working experience I had several opportunities to highlight and explore those items.

Secondly—In recent years, the emphasis on selecting leaders has grown. It seems that everyone is always seeking a good leader—tribes, organizations, companies and countries, and too often, when one is selected there follows disappointment.

And thirdly, it is helpful to recall the pleasure of working with men and women who were instrumental in accomplishing much that contributed to our society.

It is also a recognized fact that there are many in management positions that have made and/or are making great differences in the lives of people. So in this book instances will be noted in which men and women represent the various styles and manners of leadership in management and make note of the qualities that make some more leaders than others.

This book is written as an "observation", with the hope it might encourage people holding management positions to reflect on their style and methods of communicating with others.

Opening conclusions: (1) many organizations, with good purpose and intention, find themselves managed so poorly that others live at a disadvantage and unhappiness. (2) In too many instances large companies have had such poor management that millions of people have been hurt financially and otherwise and (3) In many countries on all continents, people find themselves searching for good leaders and when they don't, the results are friction and in many instances, bloodshed.

So, my question is, what is it about management and leadership that is so difficult for some men and women to accept and practice? What is the difference between a Manager and a Leader?

My Background,—As a boy, my work experience included working for my granddad mowing and trimming the properties on the two islands he built in Biscayne Bay, Palm and Hibiscus Islands, Miami Beach, selling magazine subscriptions; selling door to door roach kill; a morning newspaper route; and working as a "soda jerk" at the neighborhood pharmacy.

In my younger days there were people, men and women, who I remember as being exceptionally good leaders and role models in their positions as my parents; school or Sunday School teachers; Boy Scout leaders; store managers; Dean of Boys in High School; and in some cases, just neighbors. Many of those made impressions that have stayed with me. I am sure others have had similar experiences. I look back at the life of some of those people for inspiration.

In the Boy Scouts, there were a number of leaders who were outstanding examples of the high standards of leadership the program stood for.

During my high school years, the local pharmacist, Doc Carter, who for several years would select one of the neighborhood High school boys to work in his pharmacy, as a soda "jerk" but also to learn as much as possible about the pharmacy business, gave me a turn. I spent about one year with him after school, and remember him for his manner of teaching, helping and support in making decisions in the sale of over the counter drugs, dealing with customers, meeting delivery promises, etc.

Then there was the summer work between college terms, where I did construction work with Southern Bell

Telephone Co. in Miami. The work was hard and hot in digging ditches, laying cable and setting poles.

We had no automatic or power equipment in those days. Besides the income, I was trying to stay in good physical shape for my sport of interest, boxing. I learned a lot from the "team" leader on how to get cooperation from a group, especially when we had to man—carry telephone poles from one point to another.

This meant sometimes from a truck out front to an alley behind the homes, or the job of setting poles in the waterways, with water about a foot or so deep. The leaders' attitude, encouragement, sense of humor, and example, had a lot to do with our doing a successful job.

My personal experience with management and leadership in a large organization began when I was employed by Pan American World Airways seaplane base at Dinner Key, Coconut Grove, Miami, Florida.

In the summer of 1938, after 2 years at the University of Florida, when working with the telephone company, my mother received a call from an old friend to tell of an opening where her son, Bill Mabrey, worked at Pan American Airways. I went to their office at Dinner Key, Miami, and after an interview, was hired by the Chief, Engine Overhaul Bob Charles. It had been my intention to return to school but with this employment I put it off. At 20 years of age on August 16th, I was hired on August 20th.

So, at that age, I was given instruction and prepared for the responsibilities of planning engine overhaul schedules, communicating with the engine manufacturer, (fortunately I had learned to type in high school), working with other staff members, and about 50 mechanics and supervisors. At that time, we were overhauling

P & W engines for the PAA fleet of Sikorsky seaplanes, several small planes bringing up rubber from Manaus down the Amazon, and a small fleet of planes of ADP (Airport Development Program) in South America and Africa. (Maybe to impress the boss and to make me more comfortable with my work, I memorized the part numbers of mostly every part in the manufacturers catalog for the P & W S1EG engine used on the S42 aircraft.)

Incidentally, on my first paycheck, my high school sweetheart, Marguerite DuBreuil, and I were married and we both became part of the Pan American family. She had spent a year, after high school, working as a Postal Telegraph operator in the Pan Am Dinner Key terminal and was already close to the company and the employees. We lived in Coconut Grove and I walked to work at Dinner Key.

As we approached the war years of the 1940s, the fleet of aircraft expanded and the engines became larger and more complex. In early 1941, I was sent to the Wright Engine Factory in Patterson, NJ to aid in the administration and transfer of engine overhaul of the Wright 2600 engines (used on the B314s) from the factory to our Miami overhaul shop. My wife and I, with our new baby, drove up. Maintenance Supervisors were sent up also for technical support during the transfer. "Red" Martin was with me for 6 months and Ed Tuggle for another. In fact, my family was having Sunday dinner with Eds' family, Dec 7, 1941, when we heard the news of the bombing of Pearl Harbor.

Upon returning to Miami and the transfer complete, our office staff expanded and as we became more associated with the Military, Pan Am became a part of the Military Air Transport Command. We became responsible for maintaining and supplying aircraft with engines and parts all over the world. I coordinated my work with a military officer located at the 36th st airport.

My first real experience with supervision began at that time upon being made responsible for a group of staff employees in production scheduling and control and maintaining records of engines and components. We had to position spare engine components and sometimes engines at such places as Natal, Brazil; Accra, Ghana; Khartoum, Sudan; and Karachi, Pakistan,

During the period of 1938-41, Pan Am had a mechanics training facility on the upper floors of the theatre building in Coconut Grove, Miami. One example I remember had to do with the use of large life rafts for use with seaplanes of that era. There were regular training exercises in the evacuation of an aircraft on an emergency landing on the water which also served as tests for the rafts. At that time, the four engine Sikorsky S-42 was in use over Latin America.

I was frequently called on to select about 30 mechanics for a training flight. (The aircraft carried about 37 people) The aircraft would takeoff, then land on Biscayne Bay. The evacuation exit was out the top, toward the rear. First one out was the camera man to setup tripod and camera. Then someone threw out a 20 man life raft, then a second, and all "passengers" exited quickly and boarded the rafts. Many times the raft overturned (sometimes on purpose). And the training exercise had to be repeated.

I was impressed with the fact that the company management paid particular attention to training and testing in all aspects of its operation and full documentations was made. And it was interesting to note the improved morale on the part of the mechanics in just being a part of the training exercise.

The company President Juan Trippe, reflected such a confident attitude of exploration and expansion, and communicated these attitudes to the public and employees so well that it gave me the feeling we had a good "head of the family."
By using Clipper names he made the public feel that flying was a romantic adventure. His record of achievement and innovations is noteworthy and certainly moved Pan American to the center stage in world airline travel. It was a good feeling to be part of the team.

In our office at Dinner Key, Miami, we frequently received information and advice directly from Mr. Trippe's office in the Chrysler Building, NYC. In fact, my 3, 5 and 10 year "Pan American Airways System" service lapel pin award letter was personally signed by J. T. Trippe.

There were so many examples of outstanding leadership in all departments, corporate offices, Operations, Engineering and Maintenance, Line Maintenance, Purchasing/Supply, Medical, and others, that it would be difficult to name them as individuals.

It was a fortunate experience to work for a company, and be part of a team, where the leaders at the top were held in such high esteem by the public, and the employees were recognized for the best in quality workmanship.

My wife, Marguerite, has said many times, in our visits to stations around the world, how safe she always felt when flying on a Pan Am airways airplane. Pan American earned its reputation in worldwide aviation because of its quality of service and excellent leadership.

In my case, it was like commencing a career with a high level of expectation and confidence in company management, expecting that good leadership was the norm and always to be expected.

In later years, after studying and working with many members of management, it was clear that I could only handle that first job because of the confidence Bob Charles showed in me, the things he taught me, and the leadership skills he reflected every day. And Bob Charles was a "salesman" for top quality work and cleanliness inside the engines and on the shop floor. Incidentally, in 1939 he encouraged my co-worker in the office, and me, to join the Marine Corp Reserves along with him, and we worked on weekends to run the engine overhaul shop at the Naval Air Station at Opa-locka. In June, 1941, the Marine unit was called to active duty, but, at the company's request, we were given an honorable discharge as a "special order of the

Major General Commandant", US Marine Corp. This
was due to the fact that we were deeply involved,
working with the military, in maintaining and
supplying aircraft all over the world. However,
in 1943, I requested a leave and entered the Army
Air force pilot training program, and remained
in the program until I returned to Pan Am at the
wars end in 1945.

I retired from Pan American Airways in August
1980, after 42 years of a satisfying work
experience, with two years of military service in
the pilot training program, and having received
a BBA degree in Aviation Management from the
University of Miami. This was followed by a
comfortable but busy period of retirement in Port
Orange, Fla Incidentally, because Embry-Riddle
Aeronautical University in Daytona Beach had
visited and reviewed the Management Development
program being conducted in New York, on my
retirement I was offered an opportunity to help
implement a similar program at the university.
Although I declined, I was invited, and enjoyed,
teaching several graduate classes in Daytona
Beach. Following an active 20 years in Port
Orange, we left in 2000 and, moved into the ACTS
retirement community at Edgewater Estates, Boca
Raton, Fla.

Juan Trippe died in 1981. In 1983 he was
posthumously awarded the Medal of Freedom by
President Ronald Reagan.

Now in looking back, I am grateful for the
experience of working with such a pool of
knowledgeable and talented men and women at Pan Am.
The environment which Pan Am management provided
included good communication, and encouraged

feedback and encouragement of all employees to be creative.

In retirement years, and will refer to later, there were educating and enjoyable experiences with a Port Orange homeowner's association and the political experiences of the Planning Commissions (Miami and Port Orange), Port Orange City Council, and the retirement communities in general.

My experiences/observations plus those of others, are used without any intention of reflecting in a negative way on individuals or employers. We will consider the subject in matter alone and approach it with a positive attitude. Where we make reference to or quote material from other sources, proper recognition and credit will be noted.

CHAPTER 1

DEFINITION OF MANAGER AND LEADER

I repeat—All Managers are not Leaders. What's the difference? I have given lots of thought to this and have tried to understand and clarify the difference.

Webster defines a manager as a person who "Manages: especially, 1. a person who manages a business, institution, etc. 2. A person who manages affairs or expenditures, as of a household, skillfully and carefully".

I consider the term "management" or "manager" to include those in any position responsible for the affairs of others, all levels of management, from first level supervisor to the top level in any organization. People responsible for others affairs, business or political, are managers for purpose of comparison.

In this book, I consider a manager to be a person with a defined area of duties and responsibilities, in a variety of capacities—Supervisor, Director, elected governmental positions, City Managers, etc.

Management includes fields of sales, marketing, engineering, medical, retail and wholesale, as well as political.

Individuals reach a management position thru a variety of ways:—incidental and circumstantial;

personal desire and planning educational requirements to meet position requirements; political appointments; personal connections; organizational changes, etc

There are many managers who are very effective in the management of their defined area of responsibilities and can be proud of their achievements and progress. It is not my intention to demean or discourage them.

In fact, what I hope to do is to offer insight into ideas and methods that will enable them to grow in skills and to highlight the fact that those who extend their personalities into the area which we call "leaders" are able to leave a legacy of accomplishment in their field.

Webster defines a Leader as a person or thing that leads; directing, commanding, or guiding head, as of a group or activity"—

In this book I consider a leader as a person, usually in a "management" position, who stands out beyond the fundamentals of management; a creative thinker, willing to take a responsible risk, who considers the position an opportunity to serve others, and shows an inherent quality and style that inspires others to do well and follow him or her as an example, or follow their advice and recommendations. This is a type of person who demonstrates an ability to set goals, plan, make clearly defined decisions, and to communicate them to others with such enthusiasm that followers respond because of respect, confidence, understanding, and a willingness to follow their direction. This is done in many cases with a personality that reflects strength and with a sense of humor.

The move from a working level position into a management position, usually as supervisor, can be a traumatic move. There is no question in the fact that within the working level group, especially in a large organization, usually unionized, there is a feeling of fraternity, fellowship and brotherhood that is sometimes missing in a management group. The leadership of an organized labor group is usually the individual with a strong, forceful personality, who is knowledgeable of contracts and negotiating techniques, and has the ability to "sell" his/her ideas to their coworkers as well as management. The ability to speak clearly and with persuasive manners is one of the important qualities of the union or other labor leader. The leader has to persuade the working group to elect him/her to the leadership position. I remember union leaders who, when promoted into a supervisory position became very effective in the new position because they had demonstrated those qualities.

The term leader is an elusive term, since a leader can be a leader for good, or a leader for bad. A person in a management position can be a good "leader", with personal characteristics of a charismatic nature, but there also many examples of those who are, or were not. (Gang leaders).

A person can be ambitious and be a good leader if the goal of the ambition is to arrive at a position where he/she can apply the good qualities described above. History has shown there are many examples of strong leaders who were ambitious but had ulterior motives, selfish interests, and personal gain. That is why it is so necessary and important that individuals pay attention to the ones who present themselves as their "leader" and not follow blindly along the way.

Jack Kemp, former quarterback and Congressman, is quoted in a November 2008 newspaper article dealing with political unity, and common good as top priority, states "You see, real leadership is not just seeing the realities of what we are temporarily faced with, but seeing the possibilities and potential that can be realized by lifting up people's vision of what they can be"

There are many examples of exemplary leadership in the fields of sports, politics, and the military, but in this book we will limit ourselves primarily to the world of business management. I will, however, digress to quote a published comment by Adm Mullen, Chairman Joint Chiefs of Staff—"In battlefields and poppy fields, on trading room floors and within boardroom doors, the winds are shifting about us, once again". "But in all this, the value of leadership never changes. And it is no secret we have learned a lot from a leader named David Petraeus. His watchwords learn and adapt, have echoed from the streets of Baghdad to the halls of Washington."

The Wall Street Journal newspaper, in their November 2009 issue, included several articles dealing with "social responsibilities" in management. These articles caught my eye because they reinforce my thoughts on the importance of communication in management, be it in personal relations, the written word, or non-verbal. They made note of the fact that companies are increasingly turning to business schools to find ways to build good practices.

One article noted the fact that many companies look for new leadership by bringing in men or women from other companies where their leadership skills have proven themselves.

Most fundamental management skills can be taught, and learned by those entering a management position and can be applied effectively. Those individuals who then show the added qualities of inner strength, unselfishness, and a desire to serve others, and reflecting natural leadership qualities we consider leaders, can enhance their management skills with practice and development of many of the fundamentals. So the suggestions we discuss would be of benefit to both groups.

Peter Drucker—Management is doing things right. Leadership is doing the right things.

CHAPTER 2

WHY WOULD A PERSON WANT TO BE A "MANAGER"?

There are probably people who read this book—who think they have had no management or leadership position thus far. Some may have an interest in learning what a "manager" is, and would they want to be one.

Then there are those who have management positions to some degree but are considering giving it up.

Most people have been manager or a leader of some sort, without realizing it. In addition to the common understanding of the term "manager", for example-parents, heads of household, play ground instructors, sports player leaders, all are role models and thus leaders of those who look to them for guidance.

Many people in the workplace, however, have no desire to be a manager for a variety of reasons. Even though they want career advancement and they want more money, they do not like to have to make decisions for others and are more comfortable doing the work themselves. Many feel there is too much pressure

Example: a friend in Miami was recognized as an exceptionally good plumber and because of his high quality of workmanship, was promoted to be a supervisor. The problem was that he could not get his workers to meet the quality of workmanship he could do himself in providing service to his customers. He found supervising too stressful. So he returned to the status of a working plumber and enjoyed serving others as a first rate plumber.

Fortunately, there are individuals who observe a need and feel they can be of help to an organization, company, or country and have experience, education, enthusiasm, and/or training to offer.

Of course there are those who think they have those qualities and have a desire to control, give orders and make decisions. In other words, "be the boss" and be "in charge".

So the questions are asked?
Do you have a desire to be a manager? Do you think of yourself as a leader?
Why are you taking a course, attending a seminar or reading this book?
What are you looking for?
What are your expectations?
What new idea or method are you hoping to learn that would make you a more effective manager or leader?

Ask yourself these questions, and hopefully you will be able later to find the answers.

For someone with a desire and considering a future in management there are academic subjects which, if not included in the basic core curriculum of a desired major, are suggested to be of benefit in any field, i.e. accounting, statistics, marketing, psychology and human behavior, and especially use of computers.

Then there is question—if you are in a management position, are you a "happy" manager? Do you enjoy working with people and have a desire to be of service thru good leadership?

There are occasions where a person becomes "disenchanted" with the position he/she now holds. A person can become less effective as a manager if he/she feels that the philosophy of the company changes, when the company seems to lose its direction and purpose, its organization becomes dysfunctional, communication with other management breaks down, major personality differences with higher management, a desire to change for career interests, etc.

Then the question is—when is the opportune and proper time to voluntarily make a change?

The timing of course depends a lot on your qualifications and the state of the economy. It also depends on the level of need in the customer demand for the product you are most knowledgeable of, and especially of a known need for your skills in any specific area.

If a manager feels it necessary to make a change, it is always best and proper to cooperate with higher management in determining the timing i.e., "don't leave a company or organization in the lurch".

CHAPTER 3

QUALITIES and STYLES OF LEADERSHIP

QUALITIES—A person desiring to hold or improve in a management position can be taught and learn the basic methods of good management, but to be a truly effective and respected leader one must establish credibility, have a reputation for high ethical standards, "earn" respect, be trustworthy, and reflect an inner desire to be helpful to the group to reach a common, honorable goal.

The Sunday Chapel service at ACTS Edgewater Point Estates retirement Community, on Oct 12, 2008, offered a sermon on a subject I felt was important when discussing leadership qualities "Meek or Weak". It reminded me that many great leaders have an appearance of weakness when they are meek in nature. The word meek is most often misconstrued to be understood as weak. Webster defines it: "patient and mild: not inclined to anger or resentment."

Random thoughts—ref: Motivation
For some people, leadership and /or management skills /positions may be a means to an end . . . a mere process to insure outcomes. These people are the crusaders, even zealots, for a cause. Their commitment, passion sacrifice for their cause is their motivation . . . attributes which are contagious, often inspiring followers, even mindless followers. Defining visions, setting

goals, planning, and organizing are mechanical process left to functionaries to obtain power, money, etc to maintain momentum. The question is: what are they crusading for . . . ?

Why some people manage and lead better than others? A first thought: you'd have to look at what is "driving" someone to manage, or lead, (i.e. Eisenhower—to win a war: the Founding Fathers-to start a Nation) I question how much management/leadership, today, is influenced by ego-sustaining—greed (you see it on the news everyday: the fall of world wide financial institutions and large companies, etc) Can a person with the wrong motivation be a good manager. Maybe. Yet, I think there's a difference between being a "good" manager and a highly respected manager.

Let's not forget the word "integrity" as an almost essential part of being a good manger-leader. As an example—we might not think of a stock broker as being a manager, but because he manages other people's financial affairs, he is positively, in my judgment, a "manager".

One example—a young man, employed by a brokerage firm upon his discharge as a Navy officer in San Francisco, went thru a fine training program and did well with a growing client list. However, later, in a period of economic slump, he took it personally hard when one of his senior clients began to lose money. He found it to be difficult, after having been an advisor, to continue to be active in sale and still be honest with him self. Integrity was the key.

STYLE-A true leader needs the ability to be a strong motivator, and to develop and "sell" ideas to others in an accepted manner that encourages support and participation.

The term "leader" obviously leads to a conclusion that there are "followers". Some leaders are designated or appointed by a higher authority with the result that, even though most do, many do not have genuine followers. There are certainly many instances of politically appointed "leaders" who have as many non-followers as supporters.

Those in authority, considered good leaders, have a pleasant style of leadership through communication that creates a sense of "comfort" and confidence in the minds of those for whom he or she is responsible.

With regard to style of management—some management are the "hands on" type and feel that, in giving instructions, they must join in and help. They decide, select and monitor projects which they take great pride in and consider them personal accomplishments.

On an occasion in early 1941 when, while on a work assignment from Miami, I was in a Pan Am aircraft hangar at Port Washington, L. I., NY. The work underway was to reposition large wooden work stands beneath the wings of the large B314 seaplanes. The manager responsible was giving instructions to about 20 men on the best method. After giving instructions, he had to join in and help push. I remember kidding him, with "I thought you were the director of this operation" In the following 40 years of working with this manager, he could never keep his hands off and just direct, but he was a greatly respected supervisor. In fact, he flew with Charles Lindberg, as flight engineer, in surveying Central American routes. But his "hands on" style probably prevented his elevation to higher positions.

Another example, a supervisor in an aircraft component overhaul shop in Miami had a hard time instructing his mechanics and then leaving them on their own. He was frequently seen helping them do the work. His progression to a higher level of supervision was handicapped by that habit.

Other observations in styles—In Miami, Pan Am accomplished the overhaul of aircraft in four hangars, one for Boeing aircraft, one for Constellation, one for CV 240, and one for Douglas. An Assistant Shop Supt was designated for each type and area. The Shop Supt was one, not only to encourage, but to expect a strong competition between the areas. There was competition in meeting targets, costs, manhours, etc. All factors were measured in chart form for daily meetings and the competition was pretty serious. One Supt was known for his "hard nose" demands on personnel and thought by his challengers of "working" the books; another for his overly friendliness with personnel; another for engineering manners of running the business and the other for his "old fashioned" follow up on details. Each had a distinctive style and different manner of personality, but all were equally recognized for the effort to produce top quality results. So the differences in style proved to be an effective, overall, advantage. Those were W(pop)Smith, Gordon Cameron, Harry Steadman, and Bill Loucks.

I recall a period, in the Miami aircraft service hangar areas, there was one position, titled "General Foreman" on each work shift, considered a coordinator to assist the other supervisors in resolving problems. He was also the one person to contact for maintenance status information.

The man chosen for that position was selected for his leadership ability to gather facts, reach conclusions and make quick, correct decisions and give instructions clearly, especially in emergency periods, like hurricanes.

Example of a leader and humble attitude—One day, I had walked from my office to the security gate at Pan Am on 36th st, Miami for a "break" and when stepping inside, a man was using the telephone. He finished, turned and extending his hand, introduced himself as "Hi, I'm Lindbergh". I responded by saying," Hi, I'm Stearns". Then, noticing his build, said, if you're really Charles Lindberg, there are a lot of your friends in the hangar who would like to say hello to you. He said, he would sure like to do it but he had just made plans to visit the company Vice-Pres at his office on Delaware Parkway, he was loaned a car, and would I give him directions, which I did.

At that time he was a "leader" in the industry and his friendliness and humble attitude were noteworthy.

Lindberg and Juan Trippe

In a book titled "Leadership by the Book" by Ken Blanchard, Bill Hybels, and Phil Hodges, they pose the question "What is it that keeps leaders from being committed enough to actually use the concepts they're taught". Their research found that only a small percentage of leaders actually used the taught methods on the job and the Minister in the group wondered if people who heard sermons actually lived their lives any differently. That question gives us a lot to think about.

Other styles—from Bill Stearns—the following is a true example of, what we will call inappropriate application of "Managing by Objectives. This was a commonplace technique which assumed that all one had to do was first lay-out, and then accomplish certain "steps" needed to achieve a specific goal-and the Goal would be achieved!(a Work Breakdown Structure?) Always sounded good on paper! (Kinda like a "Map Quest" for achieving business goals) How do we get "there"—from "here"? Trouble I found was (is?) people were involved in the process. With differing viewpoints, different approaches, different motivations! Which, typically, (in my experience) meant: The only person who could layout, not only the ultimate "objective" but the "steps", too, was—the "the boss"(Which didn't make you a Manager—it made you a grunt!)!

Another quote, from Peter Drucker—"The manager is the dynamic, life-giving element in every business."

A further example, (from Bill Stearns) when introduced to "nother technique (not that I used. or use it) where the management would, sometimes almost shout at me: Stop making your dammed lists—GO DO IT! (No Work Breakdown Structure, no Management by Objectives needed, in his mind.) This produced good results.

Another word that comes to mind in thinking of style of leadership is the word "perception".

If you ask several people of what one word best describes a particular manager, you will most probably receive several different answers. How one is perceived by another is a major factor in communication. A manager can be perceived as "easy going", courteous, strong or weak, a listener, etc. Some managers, when they stand in front of a group, perceive themselves as being clear, fair-minded, a good communicator, whereas the audience may have an entirely different perspective. I have known managers who were perceived to be cold and uninterested, and sometimes too technical to be concerned about anybody's personal situation, but when you got to know them, they were completely different. So perception can make a difference.

One time I had been selected to serve on a jury and, as is the normal procedure, the jurists prepared to select one of the group to be the foreman or spokesperson. I clearly remember that one of the men proceeded to explain what our responsibilities were as jurists and the procedure we should follow. He "perceived" himself to be the leader and expected to be selected. However, he was not.

It must be understood that a retirement community is a business (some non-profit) and a director manages a staff of operations personnel but the most significant thing is that the director is not the "boss" over the residents but does control the environment wherein they live. A director—manager may have good qualities of a business nature but be wholly out of place in dealing with other peoples concerns So it is especially essential that the style of management reflect compassion and the inherent skills of good communication.

In one situation, over a period of time, a director who reflected a well accepted, personal, style of management was replaced with a more business mannered type, who was replaced by an impersonal type, who was replaced by a person with a personal style. Selection of people to management positions by senior management obviously must consider personal style an important element in making the choice.

The following are other observations of "leadership styles" based on my experience of 10 years on two Planning Commissions (Miami and Port Orange, Fl) and as member of City Council, Port Orange, Fla.

It was always interesting, when hearing a civic case of some sort, (i.e. zoning) to see the types of personalities, and the style of presentation, of the person who would come forward to speak on behalf of and represent the views of a large group of others-(business owners, neighborhood associations, etc.) They were obviously chosen by the group because of some recognized quality, (appearance, confidence and knowledge of the subject, ability to speak clearly and thought not to be confrontational but persuasive in tone, etc.) Some were "educators", who, with display material, would provide, in an interesting manner, a great deal of detail with regard to the subject. That type would, in most cases, be successful. Then there were those who were loud and forceful in tone, almost presenting a challenge to a board, who found it difficult to be unbiased and fair in judgment.

One more example—a recent newspaper described the selection of the President of Finland as a Nobel peace prize winner. The article mentioned his "style" of quiet, calm, cautious, mediator.

Further observations and experiences with different styles and methods of management—

In my earlier periods, there were visits to garment and carpet factories in Georgia and Alabama with an interest in methods of production and control. There were instances where there was noted an amazing degree of efficiency and production in what would be called a "small shop" and prior to real time computers. In visiting the Ford auto assembly plant in Atlanta during the time when the use of IBM punch cards was the means of control, there was much to be learned in management of control data.

Over a period of time, in my position as Manager/Systems/Procedures, there were visits to other airlines for the purpose of exchanging ideas having to do with methods of production information control. In visits to TWA at Kansas City, Delta at Atlanta, United at San Francisco and EAL at Miami it was always interesting to find a wide range of style, thought and methods of attempting to accomplish pretty much the same product. Different styles of management over similar activities were always noticeable, and it did not mean that each, though different, was not always as effective in reaching desirable results as others. The most valuable thing gained from this type of exchange is that improvement can be made through sharing of input from others.

Another example—the position of City Manager of a city requires all of the Basic Skills we describe in Chapter 7. Yet in my experience, as in yours, there has always been a noticeable difference in the way (style) this position is fulfilled in different cities. Realizing, of course, that the position is largely political, it has to be performed in a transparent manner, and with the full knowledge of commissions or council members as well as the general public because a good manager can provide the cities citizens with confidence and pride that the public tax monies are being properly handled.

For example, in its history, the City of Miami had experiences with a variety of manager styles and abilities. Personality differences sometimes made a great difference in public perception and in review of the history of Miami, several names come to mind who were not only "managers, but were "leaders".

Over periods of growth as in cities all over America, Miami had its share of people who were "dreamers" but also who had the inherent skills to put their dreams to work thru good management The names Flagler, Tuttle, Sewell, Lummus, and other leaders come to mind of those who were instrumental in the effective use of land, weather, money, timing, and good communication in the development and management of the city. Planning as a part of management-leadership cannot be overstated.

For example, the story of Julia Tuttle is one who, in 1893 made her plans and dreams for Miami, Fla become a reality through her power of persuasion. It was her sincere, consistent effort made to Henry Flagler to extend the Fl East Coast railways system down to Miami. She became a recognized LEADER thru her method and manner of persuasion.

My dad, Frank F. Stearns, was a LEADER of a different type. He arrived in Miami from Wisconsin in 1910 and went into real estate, followed by the development of a tract of land in Buena Vista. In 1928, as President of the Miami Realty Board, he took the lead in securing legislation to empower the City of Miami to adopt a Comprehensive zoning ordinance. In 1930-32, after a great deal of time and effort, he initiated a planning and zoning plan for the city of Miami and in 1934, with persistence, had Miami's first comprehensive Zoning Ordinance adopted. He was an active member, and panel speaker at meetings in Seattle, Chicago, San Francisco, and Washington, DC with the American Society of Planning Officials. He was invited, with others, to the White House by Mrs. Franklin Roosevelt in 1941. He directed the department of Planning/Zoning in Miami, Fla. until retirement in1958. He helped form and served as President of the Florida Planning/ Zoning Association in 1962

His style of leadership was quiet, helpful, thoughtful, and well organized. His style was not of a political nature. He provided detailed information and factual reports to the organizations he was active with and throughout his career was a well recognized leader in the profession of City Planning.

This is a reference to what may be called a "company" style of management. Pan American was recognized in the city of Miami for being a civic

minded company. For example, in 1945, after the
war I was reinstated at Pan Am as Assistant to
the Shop Superintendent, Miami. The company had
relocated most of the shops and hangars to the
land based airport on 36th st

Big Executive 1966

My dad, as Director of Planning for the City
of Miami. thought it would be a good idea to
have a view of the city from the air for the city
officials. Because Pan Am management was always
conscious of its civic image and responsibilities,
they allowed me to plan the trip. We arranged
for a DC6 aircraft just finishing maintenance
service. The invited group, including the very
popular City Manager, Dick Danner, all City
Commission and Planning Board members and staff
from the city, and newspaper photographers were
waiting at the terminal on 36th st. The aircraft
was late coming put of service, so we found a
B-307 tail wheel aircraft, out of service at
the time, on the back lot. We prepared it in a
hurry, while catering prepared a food service,
and pulled it to the terminal. Even though it

was an "old" plane by standards of the day, the company, pilots and crew made it an enjoyable and productive flight for the city officials.

This story is used as an example to show that when company management made decisions like this, it reflected "a companies' style" of management, and it not only made a great impression on the public, not as an advertising gimmick, but because the company management genuinely considered Pan Am a part of the community. It also made employees involved proud of their company. (Goodyear also did this when it gave the Miami City Planning Board free use of the blimp for aerial views during land planning)

There are many examples, over the years, of men and women, who were propelled into prominence by ideas and inventions that provided a benefit, were helpful to others, or satisfied a need, and were able to "sell" the ideas to others. These became recognized leaders in industry.

CHAPTER 4

Examples OF LEADERSHIP in MANAGEMENT

As we look back in our own experiences we can, no doubt, find examples of good leaders and then back thru history we can identify more. It is suggested that it is good for each of us to have in mind a person, either thru personal experience or thru history that you would consider above the average and the true example of a "good "leader, and someone who, when we reach a point of having to make important decisions, can wonder "how he/she would have handled this situation. Our best example is that of Jesus Christ, who lived his life reflecting qualities of leadership that demonstrated the manner and methods of serving followers.

We can agree that having good examples is a much better teacher than words alone.

It has been my privilege to have known, worked with, or for, a number of people who I remember as having demonstrated the qualities of leadership we discuss in this book and so I describe, briefly, their background and experiences.

Adding to earlier comment of my first boss, Bob Charles, the Chief, Engine Overhaul, Pan American Airways during the 1930s-1940s was a highly respected man in the field of airline engine overhaul, by the airline companies as well as the engine manufacturers. I was a newcomer to the world of business. His habit of coming in early and visiting with each department and shop and spending time talking with the supervisors and mechanics, before going to his office, kept him informed. We had a very active office staff and at the end of each day he would close up his business, come out, sit on a desk and talk with the staff while we wrapped up our business. We always went home with the knowledge of what the boss was thinking and of any thing unusual we might expect the next day.

He constantly commended each of us for good work and telling him something he did not know. He was an ex-Marine, knew the engine business, and was never fearful or worried about being exposed as not knowing everything. He was an inspirational and good example of a boss who was a team leader. Throughout my working career I remembered, and tried to emulate, his style of management.

It may be that, because I was young in my career with Pan Am, I was impressed with the quality of men who were our "senior management. It seemed to make work pleasurable and I remember the confidence I had that our company was managed well. During the period in 1938-43, when working at Dinner Key, going to work was something to look forward to.

I recall Humphrey W. Toomey, Division Manager, Latin American Division. His office was in the Aviation Building, Coconut Grove, Miami. On the occasions of my visits to his office, he was always courteous, friendly, and helpful. And he frequently found time to visit our office and shops in a casual manner. He was always considered an outstanding example of a "leader" in management.

It is good to remember the many Pan Am executives who were recognized leaders in the community at that time, the airline business, as well as motivational leaders in the company itself. For example, in addition to Humphrey Toomey, LAD Division Manager in 1951-52, there was Executive Vice President, W. L. Morrison in 1958-59, and others who come to mind that I remember, like VPs William Raven and Jim Weesner. These were executives who, along with many others, remained close to the working level employee and helped a lot with the management club in its purpose to aid in the development of future leaders. Jim Weesner is especially remembered for his being a good listener, understanding, a well organized thinker and helpful in knowledge situations.

Another was Fletcher (Fletch) Bennett—experienced as an engineer, maintenance manager, quality assurance-inspection, Maintenance Shop Superintendent (temporarily). Remembered for his quiet demeanor, philosophical broad view of any situation and as a problem solver.

There was a supervisor we called "Cowboy" Williams. In the late 1940s, in Miami, he was responsible for taking a selected crew of mechanics to a remote location, anywhere, usually in the Latin American area, where an airplane needed an engine change. He had to have a replacement engine prepared, a crew selected, special tools and equipment arranged for, loaded on an airplane and transported to the area where an airplane was in need of a replaced engine. The things I remember about him, and he was known for, were his recognized abilities for the needed items, for having special equipment manufactured in a hurry, his positive attitude in a "let's go do it", and he usually did. His enthusiasm in doing his work was catching.

Now, I would like to make reference to two other men whom I had the pleasure of knowing and working with who exemplify the qualities of leadership we speak of and who made the personal effort to grow in management and proved themselves leaders in their field. They are good examples of those who work to develop leadership qualities and, as a result, earned the respect of those whom they led.

Angelo Noa, worked with our group, in New York, as a Computer System Analyst in the 1970s. Angelo was born and raised in the Bronx, served in Army Military Intelligence, attended Teterboro, (NJ) School of Aeronautics, earned FAA License as aircraft mechanic, worked at Pan American World Airways as mechanic, then a technical analyst in Engineering/Quality/Control. While working, he attended New York University and earned a certificate in Computer Programming and Analysis. He subsequently became a Staff Engineer in Research and Development. While there, he attended Pace University at night, receiving a degree in Business Administration, major Finance. He then became a systems analyst. He was later promoted to Manager of a new department, Ground Equipment Management and then Manager of Ground Equipment Control and Analysis, responsible for a 10,000 unit world wide vehicle fleet. He later left Pan Am and served as a private consultant to manufacturers of industrial equipment. He then accepted, in 1982, the position as Director of the Office of Fleet Administration for the City of New York, with oversight responsibility for a multi-agency fleet of over 18,000 vehicles In an article, in "Public Works", by the New York

Public Works department, November 1986, Mr. Noa is quoted as saying "he believes that people are the most important factors in achieving the goals of any organization, be it private or public." He practices this philosophy by attempting to create an atmosphere of respect and trust among those with whom he deals in the performance of his responsibilities.

I feel it appropriate to include Angelo Noa as an exceptional example of a person who set goals for himself and persistently applied himself to reach the goal of a satisfying accomplishment. His well mannered disposition and confidence in working with others allowed him to be comfortable with himself and with the group he worked with.

Another example—Ray Valeika. Ray came to America from Kaunas, Lithuania as a very young man, worked to earn scholarships thru St. Louis University, Parks College and earned a degree in Aeronautical Engineering in 1964. His career as an Engineer began with Pan American World Airways, in Miami; He was later transferred with others to the new Pan Am Jet Center in New York. When an opening developed in the Reliability department, Ray was promoted to Director of Reliability. In that position he supervised a rather large staff in following and analyzing the failure rate of aircraft components and establishing a period at which a component should be replaced, time limits.

With reference to his promotion from his position in Engineering to the position of Director, Reliability, managing a fairly large group, he remembers that he had no specific training in 'people management' prior to the new assignment.

He found that his best learning experience came from reading history books, mainly Civil War, and reading about the methods of many of the officers who showed true leadership qualities. (For several years, while riding in a carpool together to and from JFK airport in New York, I enjoyed listening to Ray describe his readings from the night before. He had such a way of telling the story that I later became an avid reader of Civil War history myself)

At the time we were conducting the Management Development seminar series, Ray was always willing to take a turn at leading a seminar and sharing his experiences with others. I think that, in addition to helping, he felt it helped him learn from the experience of the other supervisors.

Ray advanced to the position of Vice President, Maintenance and Engineering with Pan Am, to the position of Senior Vice President, Continental Airlines, later to Vice President of Technical Operations at Delta, and then to Senior Vice President for Technical operations at Delta Airlines.

Ray Valeika has an outstanding record of accomplishment in airline engineering. He served as chairman of the Air Transport Association Aging Aircraft Task Force, and chaired the revision of MSG2 to MSG3 which introduced damage tolerance criteria into the development of maintenance programs. He also chaired the Engineering, Maintenance, and Material Council of ATA. He served as General Chairman of SAE Aerotech and participated in the FAA Research, Engineering and Development Committee, the Congressional Aeronautical Advisory Committee and the NRC

Greener Skies Committee. Mr. Valeika's many awards include an ATA award for leadership in the aviation industry. He was chosen by the Society of Automotive Engineers (SAE) as the recipient of the Marvin Whitlock Award for his accomplishment and long term leadership with the Aeronautical Engineering and commercial aviation industry. He has written, spoken and been quoted, on many occasions, for example-

1. Is the sky falling or is there gold in them thar hills? A viewpoint on aircraft maintenance in the US by Ray Valeika
2. Aviation Safety Alliance, Seminar on Airplane and Engine Maintenance, SFO, January 2003
3. How Far We Have Come—by Jerome Chandler in Overhaul and Maintenance, December 2003, describing Ray Valeika's thoughts on 707 maintenance.

One of Ray's speeches is included because it covers many thoughts dealing with leadership.

"Humanizing Human Factors in Maintenance"— presented by Ray Valeika, Senior Vice President Technical Operations, Delta Airlines—August 1997, conference, Vancouver, B.C. Canada.

"Good morning ladies and gentlemen. Thank you for inviting me and I'm delighted to share with you some of my thoughts on a subject of keen interest and importance—Human Factors in Maintenance.

Let's begin by making a profound recognition—maintenance people are human!! The realization of humanity has brought about all types of attribution to human factors in maintenance. We have covered under human factors umbrella everything from human resources issues, continuous job improvement programs, quality improvement and on and on. Sometimes, I feel all the soft and fuzzy issues are thrown into the human factors bucket. Human factors saves money, human factors improves morale, human factors . . . on and on.

The fact is all of these claims have some truth to them. But what I'm concerned about is that often we are deluding ourselves or hiding under this umbrella without actually dealing with the fundamental fact—human factors is all about behavior and how that behavior is manifested in operating/controlling some type of equipment. Our equipment happens to be an airplane which automatically raises the interest from mundane to the sublime.

The first practitioners of the art of human factors were aircraft designers viewing the impact of their design on the operators of their equipment. Thus a bond was formed between the designer and the operator. I'm not sure that anyone thought whether or not these design principles also formed a bond with equipment maintainers; or perhaps it was intuitively obvious that any good design must intrinsically have good maintainability principles.

Thus, much of the early human factors studies, and later conclusions, evolved from a control concept, i.e., control of a machine. With aviation growing into a transportation mode, that control aspect was expanded to a shared operation by more than just a single person, and thus, control was being shared by several individuals. So now we have two variables—people-to-machine interface and people-to-people interface. But both of these interfaces still focused on *control*. So let's examine the environment in which pilots operate and more particularly, the cause and affect of their actions

First of all—pilots operate in a confined area in close proximity to the equipment they control and in very close proximity to other pilots. In civil transports, always in close proximity to at least one other pilot.

Secondly—the causal affect of their actions most often has some direct operational impact. That is, pull the yoke and the aircraft goes up! Engage auto pilot, the aircraft flies some predetermined path. So, just like Newtonian physics, for every action there is a reaction in real time environment. I want to stress the real time environment

Thirdly—pilots generally have very repeatable and predictable activity over a fixed period of time, i.e., take off, fly to a destination and land. So, there generally is a beginning and an end, or closure, to their activity.

These three factors have played a major roll in how human factors training developed, most particularly, the role these factors play in command and control situations and /or authority over the situation issues.

Having discussed the cockpit, let's now examine the situational awareness within maintenance.

First—very often the maintenance tasks are accomplished solely by an individual. There may be a crew but they may all be doing disparate tasks. For example, and aircraft comes in for a check. You may have some folks work on engines, others lubricate and still others do the interiors.

While this may be a crew—they do not necessarily function together to control the total aspect of the operation. So while there is a person-to-person interface, it's not necessary in the accomplishment or outcome of the complete task.

Secondly, more often than not, the consequences of the task are not readily apparent.

Lubrication is a good example; in some cases it prevents corrosion, in others, it mitigates frictional forces; but in either case, there most likely is no real time cause and affect association. Maintenance tasks, especially those of preventative nature, may never exhibit their value if the problem never occurs. So you just don't know if the task is preventing a problem or if a problem even exists. So no direct feedback exists from the effort.

Thirdly—while a good deal of maintenance actions are predictable and routine, the results of these do not have closure with the completion of the task. The information about the task forms a historical record, which then is used as a basis for further maintenance action. Stated differently, the maintenance task does not end by signing off the task. It just goes into a loop of information.

As you all know, CRM began in the cockpit and it works. Since it's a success, we have had a tendency to apply it to maintenance.

The common principles or universal principles also apply to maintenance, such as assertiveness, understanding norms, managing stress, etc.

But, as you can see, the pilot environment vis-à-vis maintenance environment has some fundamental differences and our challenge is to be sure that these differences are understood and taken into consideration.

Let me sum the principle differences;

First: Maintenance can be performed singularly and is not necessarily confined to a single geographical area

Second: Maintenance may not have a real time feedback of causes ane affects.

Third: Completion of maintenance tasks does not necessarily cause closure. It fulfills a never-ending loop. Reviewing these differences, there is a common thread throughout and that is: all these activities depend on information, how it's transmitted and how it's received.

The mechanic is a transceiver of information. He receives information on what to do and transmits information of what was done. His information forms the basis of analysis, of compliance, of what works and what doesn't.

It fuels the whole maintenance process which then in turn gets back to him or her and starts again.

Indulge me for a minute, while I reminisce. When I started in 1965, life was simple. There were those that knew and those that didn't. Those that knew passed out tid bits of knowledge like a largess from above to those that didn't. We told people what to do ane we taught people what they needed to learn. Each manager had staffs to collect data and they fed him information. Very sequential, very simple and very comfortable. Organizations grew following the flow of the information: layer by layer, step by step up the pyramid, and then wisdom flowed down the pyramid. This worked rather well. We were regulated, we had a few aircraft and we replaced them at regular intervals, somewhere around 10 years. Life was good. There was no safety rating system on the internet!

In the "good ole days", the aircraft came home and we worked on them. We recognized the tail number and we knew their peculiarities.

I still remember N707PA—it always needed special trim because the wing had a permanent deformation after a pull from a dive over the north Atlantic.

Today, the role of the mechanic, especially a line mechanic, is changing rapidly. He no longer has the luxury to work through problems from beginning to end. He may never see the same aircraft twice in a month. The aircraft comes in for 45 minute turns, and they had better be off the gate, there's another one to take its place. So unless, it's a box change or something obvious, it most likely will be moved off the gate for someone else to work. The mechanic must assimilate a variety of data quickly: the log book: the crew feedback: the maintenance computer message: the bite check: the maintenance set up from maintenance control: his supervisor: the aircraft history: and probably more. Many of these are transmitted through different mediums. So we have a lot of the aircraft repairs from daytime to overnight. And here, good information is critical.

On a typical day at Delta Air Lines, we carry 305,000 people; fly about 2,700 flights (611 out of Atlanta): generate 2,000 phone calls or twx messages in maintenance control: write between 2,000/3,000 log items; and process between 8,000-10,000 records. This is on a fleet of 552 aircraft of 8 different models ranging in age form new to 20 years old.

The maintenance army moves on its data. So let's be tolerant when we hear they missed a record.

And so today's maintenance organizations are still trying to cope with a pyramidal structure or the command and control environment but information flows randomly. From all sources, all directions, vertically up, down, sideways, everybody knows something. Transmission of data has changed the world. It is changing maintenance.

How do we know if we're capturing the right data? How do we know we are sending out the right information? How do we know when and where to focus our effort?

Two dynamics have come into play. First: Information is changing the fundamental organizational structure from command and control to knowledge based.

Second: The proliferation of data is changing the maintenance process from people-to-machine interface to people-to-information to machine interface. The information variable is changing both in how we manage people and how we manage the process!

I'd like to repeat that . . . . This reality is the biggest challenge for application of human factors in maintenance.

Some of the steps we are taking are leading in the right direction. But others, like how do we control the information genie are not clearly understood nor clearly articulated. So do we go on and apply some feel good programs, hold hands and sing kum-bay-ja, or do we focus on what does a mechanic need to know?

The information genie is out of the bottle. No one has complete information, but everybody has some. How do we corral this genie: how we do abstract this random data into useful and focused information?

We have taken many steps to simplify the capture of information, but we are far from being comfortable that data is not falling on fallow ground and being lost.

We have digitized manuals (most diabolical script ever written): but other than easier access, have we improved what we tell the mechanic?

Do we have listening devices in place to understand the feedback from the mechanic? Or are we inundated with so much data that most of it is lost and never analyzed?

The beauty of making speeches is that I can throw challenges and walk away. But I also manage a world-class maintenance establishment and the challenge of understanding the human-to-information-to-machine interface is not only a challenge to you but also to me.

To be safe, we must answer this challenge. We must address the behavioral aspect of the interface. You all are working hard but are you working on the right thing

Do you know what and how to tell the mechanic? Do you know or can you interpret what he or she is telling you?

This to me is the fundamental challenge for maintenance human factors today!!! And with all the talent gathered here, it should not be an impossible task to find the correct solutions and applications. Thank you!"

Ray has allowed me to include this speech and a part of his career story as an example of what I consider one of the leadership qualities we highlight, that is "a desire to serve others" i.e. in setting and reaching goals dealing with "human safety factors in aviation."

It may be helpful to add further examples of those who have demonstrated these special qualities in their daily lives and are remembered for them.

An example of team leadership—The Sun-Sentinel newspaper of Sept 26, 2008, describes the manner in which the captain of the American Ryder Cup golf team prepared his team for the recent contest with the European team.

'Paul Azzinger divided his 12 man team into three "pods" of four players and assigned an assistant captain to each group. The group was encouraged to do more that practice together, they did everything together. All pairings came from within the group. "What we tried to do is get players to develop strong relationships with the team, Azzinger said". One of the assistant captains said it was a brilliant method of building comfort, confidence and a unifying spirit. He laid out his plan to the team at a team meeting. "He wanted to give us his vision of what he wanted to happen. All the team members, nodded their heads yes. It was seminal moment. He sold it to the team in 30 seconds." As we know, the team went on to win the Ryder Cup for the first time in 9 years.

This example represents the importance of planning, considering the values of personal relationships, accepting input, and communicating the plan to the team.

A further example—at Chapel service in the ACTS Retirement Community auditorium, Sunday Sept 28, 2008, a speaker was introduced for the purpose of his thanking our group for generous donations to his organization. He is the manager of an activity called "The Soup Kitchen" in Boynton Beach, Fla.

As he described what they do I became aware that he represents a lot of what I have wanted to say about leadership.

He and two other regular staff, with about 200 volunteers, serve food to between 200 and 1000 homeless and hungry people every day The people come from the where they live, in the woods and under bridges, for food and support. His explanation of how they operate represented—purpose, goal-setting, planning, arrangement of physical needs, organization of an activity, scheduling, coordination, follow-up, and monitoring results.

He said that many of the homeless return as volunteers after they got back on their feet. And the only requirement of the volunteers is that they "smile". The manner in which he manages the activity seemed to express true dedicated leadership thru serving others.

Peter Drucker's writings were used frequently in our management training program and I encourage others, interested in advancing in management, to read his material.

Some of the things remember about him, are (1) His principle—focus on what people can do, not what they can't. (2) His constant willingness to learn (3) He was considered humble in manners (4) He learned by asking questions (5) He was an exceptional communicator.

I was privileged to attend one of his seminars in New York City.

There are examples—where leadership qualities are recognized at an early stage. My 1938 year book for the University of Florida brings to mind several of the students who I remember as being "leaders" on campus. In referring to the Executive Council-Student Government—"if one could attribute leadership toward our present democratic system to any department of student government, it would be certainly be to Florida's Executive Council"—Two leaders of the council were George Smathers and John McCarty. Smathers later became a US Senator from Florida and McCarty was the President of the Florida Bar in 1971.

The Hall of Fame that year included Steve O'Connell, who became a respected lawyer, war hero, member of the Florida Supreme Court, and ninth President of the University of Florida. Descriptive words for him in the 1937 year book were "trustworthy, strength of character-his leadership inspires". The sports center on the U of F campus is named the Stephen O'Connell Center.

There are many others, now famous people, who have left impressions we can use as" good examples."

Martin Luther King is remembered for his ability to lead and inspire in the area where, at that time, there was a need for social leadership, especially with his famous speech "I have a dream"

Abraham Lincoln—for his courage and resoluteness—in the course of his four years, he created the role of Commander in Chief. Quote from "Lincoln's War" by Geoffrey Perret—"He also showed a natural ability to remain calm and firm when his leadership was challenged."

Ronald Reagan—is remembered for his ability to communicate. He was quoted on priorities, saying, "As you seek to change every procedure and job description to aid responsiveness, remember the bygone days when we whipped big competitors by being faster and fleeter of foot,"

A recent article about former Secretary of State Dean Acheson recognized him as a "good listener". It suggested we follow Dean Acheson's example and listen without making snap judgments. Express your concerns as questions so that you give others a chance to explain their thinking.

People continue to look for good examples in the area of political leadership. Personal qualities in individuals who are "good" managers are enthusiasm; doing helpful things for customers outside the required; using ingenuity in day to day applications (when allowed by higher management); being conscientious in meeting responsibilities and obligations.

References to others are made because it is felt that reading and learning of examples of good leadership in other people can be of benefit and a challenge to anyone attempting to do better in their own career.

CHAPTER 5

LEADERSHIP IN MANAGEMENT
FROM A WOMAN'S POINT OF VIEW

In recent years, more and more women have taken leading roles in management positions in business and government. I felt it would be interesting to understand the subject from a women's point of view, so I asked Karen Rightmire, a friend with considerable experience, to express her views and she has kindly done so . . . First, we will describe her background.

These quotes concerning Karen Rightmire are from an article by Pamela Rohland, titled "Executive Suite" in "Business 2 Business" news, Lancaster, P A, May 2002

Karen Rightmire is currently president of the United Way of Berks County—PA Referring to her early years, she was always driven by serious streak and 1960's style of passion for social issue. As a girl, she entertained herself by reading biographies of world leaders, paying special attention to those about women. The one on social reformer Jane Addams, the founder of Hull House, clinched it for young Karen. She wanted to be a social worker.

Writer's note" Until they begin telling their history to someone else, many people don't take time to observe how the ordinary extents of their early years put them on the life path they seemingly were meant to follow. Rightmire is that way"

Friendliness and flexibility are indisputably part of a United Way president's job description and she has those qualities.

She received a degree in psychology from Albright College in New Jersey, an education probably utilized every day as leader of a complex organization encompassing 35 staff members, 3000 volunteers and 41 local non profit agencies.

In an early period, having taught as classroom teacher, she said "I am better as a planner and a problem solver"

In 1971, after teaching preschool children, and doing graduate work in early childhood education, she said "Women weren't as aggressive then about pursuing their goals. If you were offered a job, you took it."

She took on supervisory roles, starting at age 23. After 19 years, she was director of community and human services, supervising 200 professional support staff and responsible for $5 million in programs serving 1350 children through the Head Start program. For much of the time, she was the only woman in senior management. She has always advocated for women in more leadership positions. "I'm vocal about it but not strident. You have to pick your battles. I'm strident about helping those with a low income."

One of her pet peeves is reading books written by a man from a woman's "viewpoint."

From a Berks County magazine titled "Living", September 2007, an article titled "Women in Business—10 women leading the way"—including Karen Rightmire, by Mary Thacker.

"For the past 18 years, Karen Rightmire has served as the president of this nonprofit organization. Karen, her 35 staff members, and 3000 volunteers have turned the organization into a place in the community for everyone, from ordinary citizens in the neighborhood to large corporations; the United Way is really a manifestation of people's lives. Karen's enthusiasm for making a difference in people's lives has made her work, as she says "both my vocation and avocation"

She has said "Everyone has a gift: the job of a leader is to find the gifts of other people".

Karen has allowed me to include a copy of a speech she gave to a Chamber of Commerce group, a business symposium, in March, 2008.

(I believe you will agree with me that Karen does have a "point of view").

"I thank the Chamber for bringing together a group of such motivated and interesting women. It's a real pleasure to be in the company of an all female group.

Most of us who serve on public boards serve with a majority of male colleagues. In my case I'm the only woman on the Vist Financial. Corporation Board of Directors, formally Leesport Bank Board, and have been for at least 13 years.

I actually got my start at being the only woman in the room at the Berks County Intermediate Unit where I served as the only woman in senior management for at least 12 years. After all this time, I've come to believe that women offer a perspective on issues that is far different than men.

We tend to jump to conclusions less quickly than our male counterparts. We are less likely to get into arguments than men are and much more likely to seek compromise.

We are more concerned with employees and their personal circumstances and will go to great lengths to make sure their interests are represented.

I also believe that we are not inclined to be competitive just for competition's sake. In other words, we are not about to get into a battle with our competitors unless there is a good reason to do so.

Men seem to have a sports or war mentality that they have to win at all costs and I don't believe women are generally like that. I think women are a great moderating factor in many ways in their board service. We certainly tend to tone down the rhetoric and particularly the language. And, we certainly bring the common sense factor to the table. Since we have so much to offer as women, I have come to think that the worst thing that we can to in an all male situation is to act like a man. My rule of thumb is not to act like, dress like or talk like them.

Back in the old days you would see women, particularly in the corporate sector, wearing gray plain suits and a little string tie. I'm sure that was an attempt to be taken as seriously as their counterparts. They made themselves invisible. Because we have so much to offer as women, the last thing we should do is make ourselves blend into the background.

One caveat here is that sexy is out. If you want to be dismissed as having little business value, come into a board meeting in low cut clothes or short skirts. Really foul language is out as well. I'm not talking about an occasional hell or damn, but I surely wouldn't go much beyond that.

Women need to pick their battles carefully in an all male situation.

There are times that you have to let something go that you would normally respond to in order to focus on the big picture. If you react to everything that happens, you will lose credibility.

Men say things to each other that many women would never say to each other. By the end of the meeting, they've forgotten all about it and are good friends again. If they were women, they would never speak to each other again.

As women, we need to learn to let things roll off our backs and not to take things as personally in the board and corporate arena as we might in a different situation. The trick here is to be respected and seen as smart, competent and one of the team without being seen as to prissy or prudish. You want to be one of the team but not one of the boys!

I am very clear that I was asked to be in the Vist Financial Company's board and holding company because they needed a woman. I have this vision in my head that all of the men sat around the board table and finally came to the conclusion that it would look better for the bank if they had

a woman on the board. Who should that be . . . .
we need someone that has a good reputation for
integrity, name recognition and someone that we
can get along with.

I am also relatively certain that there are
others of us here tonight that were invited for
the same reason. The truth is that while we were
invited for this reason, all of us now play
leadership roles in our board positions.

Once you break through the barrier of
being invited to be on a board, preparation,
participation and being able to help the company
achieve its goals, will put you in a leadership
position.

- -

I am also including a portion of an address she
gave in a Commencement Address to the Alvernia
University on December 14, 2008.

After noting many of the historic events
which had occurred in her lifetime to date, she
said—"All of these events shaped many of us into
people who wanted to go into helping professions.
Many of us who went into human services became,
mostly unbeknownst to ourselves, servant leaders.
What's that?

A fellow named John Greenleaf coined the
phrase. In a nutshell, servant leaders start
with a natural feeling that they want to serve
first and then aspire to lead. This kind of a
leader first makes sure that other' priorities
are met. I'm quoting him here, "The test of
servant leadership is, do those being served
grow as persons, become healthier, wiser, freer,

more autonomous or more likely themselves to be leaders?. Will the least privileged benefit or not be further deprived?"

This is not top-down leadership but depends on collaboration, teamwork and employee empowerment. This is the kind of leadership ideally suited for the running of helping organizations and, as time has gone by, been adopted by many corporations."

Train for management—

Strive for leadership

CHAPTER 6

ORGANIZATION—

Webster's definition:—a body of persons organized for some specific purpose—

Quote—There are great examples of "good" management organizations and processes with "bad" managers . . . and "bad" management organizations and processes with "good" managers.

It is an obvious fact that every company, association, unit, etc operates with some form of organization. Communication within an organization must clearly define responsibilities, roles, and expectations. There must be a means of effectively communicating to those involved in the accomplishment of the product. Design of the organization depends on functions, numbers, product, goals, etc.—
—Forms of organizations are depicted thru "organization charts".
A line organization shows the relationship between superior and subordinate. A lateral chart shows relationship between departments on the same hierarchical level.
A staff charts reflects relationships between a manager and managerial assistants who have no authority over operational functions.
A functional chart shows relationships between specialists and other areas.

I will use two examples of organizations with which I am fairly knowledgeable of, Pan Am and the ACTS Retirement Community

Pan Am's organizational chart was primarily functional, depicting the working relationships between departments. Pan American Airways was formed in 1927, with flights from Key West., Fla. to Cuba. Its Goal was clear—to provide air transportation to the traveling public. It grew over the years, with a constantly expanding market of locations around the world, and new types of aircraft, from seaplanes to double-decker land planes. The numbers of personnel, skill requirements, and styles of management required grew, along with the physical growth.

My recollections, while in Maintenance Procedures, are of frequently revising organization charts and rewriting of duties and responsibilities at all levels. Elements of an organization chart, i.e. line, lateral, staff and functional must necessarily be kept current, clear and representative of the proper relationship between all levels.

A chart is recognized primarily as a "formal" relationship but the effectiveness of the operation depends on the managerial style and methods of communications between the levels. For example, Pan Am had large numbers of personnel stationed at such a wide range of locations that there needed to be good understanding of responsibilities and the "chain of command" authorities for effective decision making.

A quote from one of PAA's employees in overseas station management, Miller Logan—"The management of Pan Am's station locations over the period I was with the company was a moving target and differed considerably from one period to the next. An interesting subject in just comparing the merits and demerits of different approaches. Providing a happy relationship between functional and administrative responsibilities was always a challenge."

Because of the structure of Pan Am, with such a variety of required skills, the company offered many opportunities for personnel with certain skills to transfer to other departments and/or locations, some in far countries, as a part of the companies needs or to assist those countries with their airline development. For example, there were needs for staff from Maintenance and Engineering, Production Control, Supply, etc to places like Rio de Janeiro, Brazil, Zaire, Congo:, Kabul, Afghanistan, Goa, Portuguese, India, and others.

Organization and reorganization are obviously necessary as companies grow and expand and so management must be close enough to employees to realize that the lives of company personnel are affected. Pan Am was always known for its consideration of the effect of moves on its personnel.

When Pan Am relocated from Dinner Key, a seaplane base, to the Miami land airport there were many changes, then more changes resulted from the closing of a Brownsville, Tex. base and the resettling of personnel to Miami. During the late 1950s-and early 1960s, top management wrestled with the question of whether to continue Miami as the main base or to move to New York.

During that period, as Manager, Systems/ Procedures, my responsibilities included a program to install data gathering computer devices throughout the Miami hangars and shops. It was going well and we were continuing to develop informational reports for management when I was requested to move to New York to plan, install equipment, and provide similar reports for New York management.

At time of the first request to move, we had two sons in local schools and we felt it would not be good for the family to move. So we declined. The company allowed me to continue in Miami while spending a lot of time commuting back and forth to New York. However, the Miami operations continued to slow as department activities relocated. So, in 1968, the sons had completed local schools, so we made the move to New York. Actually, in the long run the move was to our advantage. My wife and I were exposed to a broader perspective and social life, financial incentives helped with the higher costs, and my opportunities on the job expanded. The point is, during the period of transition, PAA management was very considerate of people and their individual situations, in all departments, and very rarely were people forced to move. Many continued in Miami until their retirement.

The leaders of Pan American Airways made many decisions over the years that were significant and of major benefit to America and its friends all over the world.

A book titled "The Chosen Instrument" by Marylin Bender and Selig Altschul describes the Rise and fall of an American Entrepreneur. It tells the story of Juan Trippe, his leadership qualities and of pioneering Pan American Airways, which for more than half a century was America's most powerful international airline Pan Am's continued development as a leader in world wide aviation and the amazing technological changes which took place during that period, allowed the company to serve as a recognized "ambassador" to other nations as they strove to develop. It was always with pride that a person could say "I work for Pan Am".

From my personal experience and point of view, there were two periods where top management decisions made a major difference.

In the 1960s when the company was trying to decide whether or not to move the main base from Miami to New York. A former PAA pilot was President at that time and, after much deliberation of important factors, the decision was made to move to New York. It seemed that most all employees had an opinion at that time, and of course the Miami people thought it would be wrong. It seemed to Miami people that the "roots" of the company had to do with Latin America and labor relations were good in Miami, where' as, at New York the unions were more aggressive and cost were high. The pros were that the company was focusing more on global operations and the JFK airport would be a better location. The move had a traumatic effect on everyone. Construction of the JFK jet center was a major, costly project, but operations did expand from that point so history will have to determine whether or not it was a good decision.

Another major decision made by PAA management had to do with the adding of National Airlines to the PAA system in the 1970s. Pan Am's international traffic was being affected by the fact that we had helped so many of the worlds countries to begin operating their own airline that it did affect the company's traffic so Pan Am decided it needed to connect with a US domestic carrier to feed traffic to its international routes.

The ACTS Retirement-Life Communities, Inc. was formed over 35 years ago, to set a standard in retirement living, with a vision founded in faith and guided by a commitment to integrity and loving kindness. From humble beginnings in Pennsylvania, ACTS has grown to 19 communities in six states. Management has expanded and has become more complex, in accordance with the need of geographical location growth and typifies "span of control" changes. ACTS organization chart would best be described as "locational" and personnel oriented.

This example, on the subject of "span of control" is offered by Walter Arnold, a 25 year former resident of the ACTS Retirement Community. (Walter's experience included 46 years in the field of vocational education). "The span of control in a corporate organization might be described as the range of management between the Executive officer and the first level of supervision. To illustrate, ACTS, a non-profit Life Care Retirement Community, headquartered in Philadelphia, PA now operates 19 facilities in five states-Penn., Florida, Georgia, North and South Carolina and Alabama. When ACTS was founded 35 years ago, the span of control was one to one. Today the span is 1 to 19.

It is obvious that ACTS must now clearly define every level of management with job descriptions and responsibilities fixed at every level. Communication throughout the span is of great importance. It is a difficult task in a large corporation with a long span of control. One device used to overcome problems arising in a large span of control was a practice used by Armstrong Cork Co, a very successful corporation in Lancaster, PA. The President was a very able manager. In 1935 he employed a young Industrial Engineer, graduate of Purdue U. to become his plant wide "advisor". The advisor was given every freedom throughout the plant as a kind of troubleshooter. He was authorized by the President to talk with any level of management about a troublesome situation. He was given access to the Presidents office at any time to communicate the problem to him. It was kind of an open communication system from first level up to the President. It proved to be very successful in developing a smooth management system."

CHAPTER 7

DEVELOPMENT OF MANAGEMENT-LEADERSHIP SKILLS

When we discuss management, it should be understood that I am not attempting to write a "How to" book". There is a wide selection of books written by knowledgeable authors on this subject.

It seems appropriate however that in any discussion on this subject, where I relate experiences of good management and the special qualities of, what is defined as leadership, I should offer some suggestions for self improvement.

Many people promoted from the ranks into a management position had received no preparatory training in the skills necessary or at least helpful in the management of people.

It is a recognized fact that those who enter management by way of a promotion from the ranks are usually selected based on recognition of good workmanship, dependability, and knowledge of the product or process. (For example, those promoted from mechanic to supervisor, clerk to office manager, salesman to sales manager, or engineer to Director).

Others enter management from the outside by academic credentials

In my recollection, most management positions at Pan Am, at least in Maintenance & Engineering, were held by those with considerable background in mechanics and others with Aeronautical, Mechanical, Electrical and other related engineering degrees.

As one of the men promoted to a supervisory position in Miami in the 1940s recently remarked, "I was appointed, pinned, and told to go". It should be noted however, that in the selection process, those promoted were recognized as having demonstrated natural and comfortable leadership qualities among the crew they worked with and had the ability to learn many of the skills of management; they did adapt to the responsibilities, and did well as supervisors.

It should be remembered that we are writing of "people" training and not "technical" training. Pan Am was always recognized in the industry as being of the highest quality in workmanship because of its long and continued program of technical training.

In speaking of skills concerned with the business of managing people, and in the process of promotions, I am assuming knowledge of the product or process at the time of selection for promotion.

My experiences in management development are included as "suggestions for consideration".

Educational opportunities for personnel at Pan Am were offered and encouraged over the years, including a variety of subjects. Much of it was provided with the support and coordination between the company and the PAA Management Club. The clubs purpose, as an educational service, was designed to broaden the individual's understanding and appreciation of management, its problems and solutions.

· The club sponsored courses in conversational Spanish, public speaking, industrial psychology and other subjects of general interest. Monthly meetings included guest speakers from the Miami business community as well as Pan Am senior management and, on frequent occasions, company pilots and other operations personnel. Those meetings provided a major and inspirational benefit in good communications throughout the company. Financial support was provided through the Management Club in Miami for scholarship assistance at local universities.

In a letter in 1959 to. Bob Thibert, President, PAA Management Club,. W. L. Morrison, Executive Vice-President, Latin American Division, with reference to the value of the club, stated "That purpose is to establish firmly the PAA management Club as an organization to assist its members in gaining better understanding of the principles of business and the promotion of good influence and fellowship in the community."

I found a lot of satisfaction and benefit in the club's programs, was active in various capacities, and served as Secretary during 1951-52; Chairman, Scholarship Committee 1956-57; Member Board of Control 1960-61; and Junior Achievement Advisor 1966-67.

Pan Am also had an Executive Training Program where a limited number of individuals were selected by department heads and were scheduled to visit and work with most other departments throughout the company. But that training was primarily to become familiar with the various aspects of the company.

Management encouraged all personnel to continue helpful educational programs, and supported us in many ways. Since at that time, I had completed two years at the University of Florida, I was encouraged to continue studies at the University of Miami so I attended school nights and weekends with the help of the GI Bill.

It may be of interest, because it relates to a manner of managing a project, to describe the program at the University of Miami. The U of M was initiating a program of Aviation Management to compare with a well recognized program being conducted at Purdue University. It coincided with the interest of Pan Am personnel who were attending school to gain more knowledge of aviation management. The well educated professor, responsible for the program, took advantage of the students with aviation experience.

He broke the class into groups, with each assigned to prepare a "chapter" on the various aspects of aviation taking place at the Miami Intl airport. I was assigned to write a chapter on the handling of the many small, private and commercial aircraft, operating in and out of the airport while not interfering with the operation of the large airline aircraft. Even though I was working down the airport with Pan Am, I had not paid particular attention to the manner and methods of handling arrivals, servicing, catering, dispatching of small aircraft. I was treated cordially by the managing operators of the many aircraft. The material I learned was discussed in class, along with the material brought in by other groups. In effect, we were preparing a "text book" for future classes. It was truly an interesting and practical manner of teaching a subject.

I received a Certificate in Basic Aviation Administration in 1955 and graduated from the University of Miami in 1957 with a degree of Bachelor of Business Administration-major Aviation Management. Because of my studies in aviation management I was asked to, and enjoyed, conducting seminars at PAA on a variety of subjects relating to company administrative procedures.

In 1956, I received a "Certificate of Recognition" from Division Manager Raven for a presentation on the subject: "The LAD Maintenance Department" as a part of a successful Maintenance Conference Program.

I was also honored with a certificate for taking part in ongoing training programs for Maintenance & Engineering-

Pan Am Maintenance & Engineering

proudly presents to

John M. Stearns

a

Performance Merit Award

for his dedication to the task
of educating technical personnel
in the art of management,
encouragement for self development,
positive effects on our social
attitudes at work and assistance
in shaping our leaders for tomorrow.

Reference to these certificates is made to help make clear my involvement and interest in

Management Development/Supervisory Training over most of my career.

I was also fortunate to have had an opportunity to attend a "systems" convention in Philadelphia, a seminar at Columbia University in New York, and several conferences in New York City dealing with administrative procedures.

While in Industrial Engineering, working with Tom Peters, I enjoyed having to identify a problem with a work item procedure or process, and suggesting a better way of doing it. We did a lot of study with methods of problem solving. This brought me into an ongoing working relationship with maintenance supervisory personal and learning their manner of work assignment and follow up for job completion. I found it helpful to observe the relationship between mechanics, supervisors, and upper management.

At that time there was a realization that computers would be a tool of the future, so management allowed me to take a group of supervisors from Maintenance, Engineering and Supply, to attend a course in the fundamentals of computers at the Charron-Williams Business College in downtown Miami. In May, 1968, after completing the 16 week seminar, we received a Certificate in Data Processing for Management. That was a very helpful basic training program and was the beginning of my involvement with computer systems design and allowed for the inclusion of supervisors of all departments in future computer applications. IBM was very cooperative and frequently provided films for training personnel in the fundamentals of computers. From that point, I was involved in a project of installing data collection devices throughout the hangars and shops, and designing

computer programs to report various informational
reports, until my transfer to New York later in
1968.

During my time at the Jet Center Pan Am base
in New York I was fortunate to manage a group
of Computer Systems Analysts, for the purpose of
continuing the installation of Data Collection
devices through out the shops and hangars, and
design computer programs to meet the needs of
management in the various departments. We were
following the approach that had been taken in
Miami. I discuss this further in the chapter
titled "Project Management".

In the late 1970s, in New York, at a point in my
career when the installation of data collection
equipment and the design of new computer systems
had tapered off, I had been assigned to the
training department to conduct various programs
to train personnel in the most effective use of
the computer systems currently in use.

Working with Director Bill Manners, along with
the highly skilled technical trainers in that
department taught me a great deal about methods
of instruction. For example, the use of photos,
film developing, and graphics. Along the way I
conducted several classes for Purchasing Dept
personnel to help in use of current Purchasing
computer programs. For background, in June,
1975, I completed a 19 hour American Management
Association course titled "Fundamentals of
Purchasing for the Newly Appointed Buyer".

While in the training department, it became
clear to me that a large number of management
personnel would be planning retirement in the

near future, especially the large number who had been transferred from Miami to New York about the same time. With that fact in mind, and having worked so closely with supervisory personnel for so many years, I developed an outline for a "Management Development/Supervisory Training" program and submitted it to Management. The plan was approved and I was allowed to plan and conduct a program with the support of all departments.

It may be helpful to describe the program we used at Pan Am, and supplement it with educational material offered by experienced friends and former coworkers. In preparing our program I read lots of material on the subject, and interviewed many upper management personnel, supervisory personnel, and learned of problems and needs. I received full cooperation from my Director, Bill Manners and the staff of the training department as well as upper management from all departments.

Most of the program at Pan Am was conducted in a classroom style, but the basic skills are applicable by individuals with a desire to learn and or improve.

Our program did not cover, in particular, all the skills considered important however I will describe some of the subjects we did include and will expand the subject material to include information from additional sources.

In this program, we offered two approaches. One we called "outhouse" where we assisted personnel in analyzing their educational needs and suggested certain local college programs which could be of help and could be used with as little inconvenience to work and family life as possible.

The other was an "in-house" program and consisted of seminars and classes on the following subjects:

A. seminars

B. Communication
C. Speaking
D. Listening
E. Speed Reading
F. Meeting Management

G. Budget Planning/ preparation
H. Delegation
I. Personal Dynamics
J. Training.
K. Performance Evaluation
L. Adding new employees

A. Seminars

A series of Seminars—One to two hour seminars held weekly, with 12 to 14 Supervisors, Managers or Directors. The primary purpose was to motivate and inspire our management personnel to prepare them for advancement. However, for those who had not had prior management/supervisory training, it "opened the door" to a full view of their responsibilities and opportunities. Participants were selected by Department heads and though, organized by me, as Manager, Management Development/Supervisory Training, each session was lead by an invited Director or Vice-President. Some were from the corporate office in the Pan Am Bldg. Each discussion leader was asked to describe the method he/she found most useful and helpful in reaching the position now held. Each participant was encouraged to express his or her views, questions, problems, and concerns and it usually became an active, interesting discussion session. I received and used copies of a Harvard Business Management Review paper as subject matter for discussion material. Response and feedback proved the program justifiable and beneficial.

In conjunction with the seminars, a curriculum of, what we call primary skills, was carried out in classrooms.

B. Communication

It had always been my belief that good, clear communication within an organization and with those outside the company is a major key to success in all good management. This was based on my early experiences with Pan Am management. Therefore I included several forms of communication in our program. Classes were held on Communication Skills.

Communication in management employee/or other relations is too often thought of as primarily oral and written. In my preparation, in August, 1979, I completed a course offered by the English-Language Institute of America, Inc, titled
"Practical English and the Command of Words"

The written word is, of course, a necessary means of communicating an organization's mission, goals, priorities, and procedural methods of establishing and maintaining order within the organization. When these items are developed, with input and support from those subjected to them, they provide a basis for clear common understanding.

However, Non-verbal communication is too often overlooked in speaking of the subject. In discussing non-verbal, I am referring to, what is probably the most important factor on the subject of communication. Facial expressions are a common form of non-verbal communicating. Smiles, scowls, smirks, look of concern, questioning are forms frequently experienced. When a doctor makes a test of some sort, and reflects a facial expression of concern, it naturally causes a patient to fear the worst. When a senior manager enters a meeting, with a scowl, and sits without saying a "how are you or good morning", it allows a feeling of discomfort among the participants. When the "boss" walks into the office in the morning and if he/she walked straight to his/her office without speaking, smiling, or acknowledgment in some form, to the staff, what would he/she be communicating? It would surely leave concern and uncertainty on the minds of the staff.

Many times, the attitude of those in a subordinate relationship is reflected in the manner in which management personnel appear in contact with a people in the organization. A management person passing a person in the hallway or hangar floor without speaking, or careless sign, is "communicating" an attitude of superiority and not caring and certainly not showing a desire to learn how a person feels.

Example: at one time a Shop Superintendent, (although highly knowledgeable technically) would walk across a hangar floor without speaking to any of the mechanics. A simple hi would have been helpful to morale. There was a recognized lack of interest in his future.

A major means of communication between management, of any level, and employees or staff is by personal example, demonstration of knowledge of the "business" of the organization, willingness to share information, manners, clear sincerity of purpose, and a sincere indication of a desire to accept "feedback" from others.

For example the Director of Engineering at PAA, Norm Smith, in Miami, frequently held informal discussion sessions with the staff, one of which was to explain his understanding of the effects of lightening on aircraft in flight. Sessions like this built an appreciation of his interest in sharing knowledge and earned respect.

Communication with a person in higher management can be difficult sometimes. It is well for a subordinate to learn the habits and interests of those he/she reports too. When a subordinate goes into the bosses office when he/she has something other on his mind, the subordinates' needs or ideas don't receive high priority. Timing is important and, when thoughtful in this area, it demonstrates the subordinates desire to be helpful and cooperative.

Communicating with upper management is best accomplished with brief graphic facts and presentations.

It is extremely important that the "boss" be kept informed of problems which could be embarrassing if he/she is not knowledgeable of an issue, especially in financial matters. Each level of management should, of course, take steps necessary to solve problems but just don't leave the "boss" uniformed.

Over the years I had many occasions to use flip charts or overhead projectors in making presentations to management. This was the age, prior to PowerPoint computerized methods, where there was a lot of conversational exchange during a presentation, and I enjoyed the comments. It was always important, and interesting for me, to watch the faces of senior management, while I was providing a presentation either on screen or flip charts. Sometimes a look of doubt or questioning made me get ready for some "back up and support". Non-verbal.

"For workers and bosses, communication needs to be a two-way street". That's a headline in a local newspaper today (Sept 25, 2008). The story deals with a large furniture company that has become aware that communication was even more important in uncertain times. Manager's and employees gather to have an" ultimate update" each morning. They realize that employees who are fearful are less willing to speak and tell mangers what's really happening at the company. They realize that both employers and workers have responsibility in this climate, experts say.

The importance of communication in management has been strongly reflected in recent articles (2009) in the Sun-Sentinel newspaper in Florida. These well written articles, by Marcia Pounds, caught my attention because they emphasize some of the points I found so important in my training programs.

One article, titled "When workers talk, the smart managers listen", speaks of "appreciation as a way of motivating employees and refers to typical comments from employees like—"my employer doesn't help me further my career", "I'm not happy in my job" and "he's not working as much as I do". Managers who listened and responded to questions and comments, by, in some instances taking self improvement courses, reported noticeable improvement in departmental morale.

Another article, titled "Communication is key to winning over your boss" includes quotes from a local university management department professor which highlight (1) Learn your boss' communication style, (2) be proactive, (3) meet regularly, (4) ask for your bosses opinion, and (5) go to your boss with solutions. Another article by Marcia Pounds in the Sun-Sentinel, reported the fact that a CEO of a company had received a "worst boss" rating, indicating that the rating usually has to do with lack of communication.

An example—in reflection. In early days Pan Am had a reputation for quality of workmanship. One of the reasons was that the Chief Engineer, Andre Priester, used to come from NY to Miami and visit the mechanics in the engine shop and listen to their opinions and discuss quality. He was a good communicator and there was always a high degree of morale. In later years, VP and Chief Engineer, John Borger, also was recognized for his ability to communicate.

In companies where the work force is unionized, it is extremely important that management at all levels learn the importance of good communication. There needs to be a formal manner (i.e., scheduled meetings) but most important, an open and informal manner of keeping in touch with the feelings of the employees.

All management personnel must be knowledgeable of written agreements with the authorized unions and avoid any instances or problems because of misunderstandings or lack of proper knowledge. Example, there were several occasions when labor problems resulted when a supervisor was not aware of a provision in the contract that been allowed the Union Chief Steward, and a strike occurred. When there were walkouts, it was then that communications at all levels was extremely important. It is always hoped that negotiations between unions and management will proceed smoothly, and they will if communications channels are kept open. The fact has to be remembered that the aim of management is to maintain loyalty of employees while realizing there is a split loyalty shared with the labor organization. The purpose in good communication is to avoid conflict and provide evidence of trust by both parties.

There was a period where Pan Am in Miami accepted the support of an organization titled "Moral Rearmament" MRA, where the purpose in working with the labor group and management was to establish a basis for trust in each other.

The method of Communicating has obviously evolved over the years from oral, written, telephone, to electronics (email) and conference meetings with computers etc.

The following is noted as an example of, what can be considered an effort at good communication by the ACTS Retirement Community management, from Corp headquarters office in Penn. A letter addressed to each of the approx 8000 retiree/residents in six states, in an Oct 6, 2008 letter signed jointly by the President and Exec Vice President/CFO, described and answered questions pertaining to the effect of the national financial crisis on each of us and plans to "provide you with a full explanation, on or prior to Nov 1, which addresses and supports the need to adjust monthly fees". The information was not processed thru other layers of management, on this subject, and although not necessarily good news, it appears to be an honest attempt to clearly communicate.

Now let's review some other basic methods of communicating.

C. SPEAKING

It is more important than ever, in this day and age, that a person in a leading position be able to speak clearly and comfortably. A speaker must be able to present a subject in an understandable and believable manner, because, in most cases, the leader is attempting to persuade followers to accept a belief. It is important that those being spoken to, co-workers, employees or the public, hear honesty, knowledge of the subject, trustworthiness, and sincerity of purpose

There are many books on the most effective manner of speaking to individuals or groups. In a course I took at the U of Miami on speaking, I felt that I benefited by support and response from the class so I worked to develop that approach.

It might be helpful to relate my personal experience with "public" speaking. In the early period of my involvement with the PAA Management Club, I was frequently asked to give an opening prayer for the group of probably 100-300 people in somewhat formal setting. Even though I had prepared my thoughts, and I knew most of the members, when I was called on, I would "freeze" and find it difficult to express my thoughts comfortably. I had "stage fright". With help, I learned to overcome the problem by continuing to do it. Books on the subject stress the need to practice by doing. I found it very helpful for later experiences.

Speaking to an individual or an organization should obviously show sincerity of interest in an exchange of views.

Speaking to a group should reflect appreciation to the attendees, outline of purpose, necessary background, (in brief), time limitations, definition of any problem with suggested solutions, plans and provisions for change, encouragement of response and listener input and conclusions.

When speaking to an audience, it is always helpful that the speaker make certain he/she is reaching those in the rear of the group. And if not sure, ask those in the rear if they can hear clearly.

When leading a seminar, with expected sharing of thoughts, it is always helpful to call on, by name, any individual who had not expressed an opinion to that point. Many very intelligent people are, by nature, quiet and reluctant in expressing opinions. I found that to be true in some of our more qualified engineers.

In a group training setting it is always helpful to have each attendee take a practice turn, and speak on a subject requested by the moderator. It offers a benefit in having to think and speak on an unfamiliar subject. In our classes at Pan Am, we tape recorded each speech and, in replaying, found that supervisors gained confidence in their ability to communicate with others.

D. LISTENING

Individuals assume they are hearing what is being spoken. An individual can learn and practice the importance of listening and actually hear and sense the intent of the person speaking. When a manager is listening to an employee, he/she should make a sincere effort to pay attention to the attitude of the speaker, and try to hear the "inner" feelings being expressed. This is where non-verbal communication comes in play

A simple example—many people, after an introduction cannot remember the name of the person introduced. It has been suggested that when introduced, the "listener" repeat the name with a friendly question.

Peter Drucker said—The most important thing in communication is hearing what isn't said.

According to one of his secretaries William Stoddard, Lincoln was an exceptional listener. "He was a most teachable man, and asked questions with a childlike simplicity which would have been too much for the false pride of many a man far less well informed. His fund of knowledge was, as he himself declared, very largely made up of information obtained in conversation."

Secretary of State Dean Acheson was known to be a good listener and to allow his aides to support their recommendations. He encouraged free and open comment and listened well before judging.

E. SPEED READING

In my last year of studies at the University of Miami, I took a course in speed reading. I found it very helpful and wished I had been able to take the course in the first year. It gave tips on broadening the readers view, determining need for following info from first line of paragraph and many other helps

In our PAA program, with a purchased program of several books to read for specific benefits, some technical as well as narrative, it provided a benefit to management personnel in reading more quickly while at the same time learning more of the material.

In reading technical material it usually helps to run your finger along the lines, slowly for heavy stuff, faster for lighter.

When reading material of a technical nature, make sure you understand the intent and purpose for your reading. Sometimes, for subjects outside material of your expertise, you can get into the detail before thinking of the overall purpose and what you are expecting or hoping to learn. For example, if reading about solar energy or wind turbines, etc, preview the introductory and summary information, and form questions in your mind of what you are looking for. Response to our program was positive and most students found the course to be of benefit.

A young man who, attending the Naval Officers Candidate School in Rhode Island, had an exam on nuclear energy scheduled in the week following a weekend leave. On the weekend leave, he had the book, and between social events, read/studied the book, and on his return to school, took the test and did very well. He had the ability to read what he considered necessary to understand the subject for test purposes.

During recent months (2009) much has been said of the voluminous bills and amendments US Congressional Representatives and Senators are called upon to be knowledgeable of and able to vote on. The excuse most often heard was the many pages required to read in a short time. The ability to speed read would have been of value.

The method of communicating has obviously evolved over the years from oral, written, telephone, to electronics (email) and conference meetings with computers etc. Each of these methods should be understood and used to best advantage.

F. MEETING MANAGEMENT

Managing or directing the affairs of others requires good communication. There are of course a variety of ways to do this—as mentioned earlier—but bringing the participants together at some point is important for a face to face period of conversation to give instructions, question those involved, learn status, etc. Types of meetings vary greatly. Public hearings, schools, PTA, company, organizational, etc Meetings-remember, are for the overall purpose of communicating. So remember meetings are for the overall purpose of communicating.

Meetings are generally of three types (purposes).

1. to provide information—maybe from senior management or having been requested to be presented by one of the participants.
2. to give direction—may be a revision in company policy, procedure or method.
3. to learn—may be called to learn and share status of projects for which participants re responsible.

In the world of business, the ability to effectively manage a meeting is extremely important in being an effective manager, and there are certain basic things to consider.

This subject includes:

A. *Planning the meeting or seminar.*

   1. Define purpose and goal
   2. Develop agenda
   3. Determine number and purpose of participants.
   4. Determine/confirm location
   5. Arranging (resources)

      a. accommodations i.e. seating
      b. food/drink
      c. Provisions for graphic display,
      d. Travel planning
      e. Informing participants of plans.

(Business meetings, especially when it is a "boss" or company scheduled meeting, are usually held in a conference room, frequently at a remote location. In these instances the amenities are prearranged)

B. *Conducting the meeting*

   a. Introductions
   b. provide agenda
   c. define goal and expectations
   d. Inform attendees of expected closing time and work to stay on schedule
   e. Sometimes ask for questions at opening.
   f. encourage discussion while being a good listener.
   g. Controlling
   h. Closing

C. After meeting conclusions and communicating results to those interested and concerned.

Remember, there is a responsibility for serious attention and preparation on the part of those invited to be participants in a meeting. A participant who attends but offers no info, no comment, no question and leaves without having commented has contributed nothing to the meeting. He/she may have learned something or known something but the person chairing the meeting and other participants would not have known it.

The following is a response to the question "what leadership qualities are needed to moderate a group" brought together in some common interests. This particular situation was in reference to a "Divorce Support Group" conducted by my son Bill.

Be prompt—start meeting on time. (I found out that if I didn't people would get in the habit of wandering in late.)

1. As a moderator—"listen" more than talk.
2. It is necessary for me to police—in a nice way—the amount of time each individual has to "tell 'bout their situation". (There have always been those who felt they could: hog" the entire evening—with no consideration for others.)
3. Don't hesitate to ask those (who are there for the "wrong" reasons-like: looking for somebody to date)—to stop attending!
4. Keep meetings . . . moving!
5. Have some sort of "hand out" that explains the "rules" of the group.
6. Provide a (typed out) general "topic" of discussion. This prompts those who are

"shy" to talk and, to contribute to the discussion.

7. End meetings on a bright note"—with an uplifting story or, comment, (sometimes a' little humor.)

8. End meetings—on time! (the best I can)

In my career, there were many occasions to plan and conduct meetings. Many were company type or training meetings, but there were several other occasions.

For example, my turn as Chairman, Miami (Fla) City Planning and Zoning Board came in 1962. Having served on the board for 6 years, evenings, I felt that I knew each member well enough to develop an idea I had for managing the meeting in a better way.

We rotated the Chairmanship each year and when I took my turn, I had an idea I thought would help shorten the always long and late meetings. Meetings usually ran until midnight or later because applicants for zoning changes wanted the hearing. My suggestion was that each member, when commenting on an agendas item, limit himself/herself to approximately 10 minutes. The response from the group was overwhelmingly opposed to the idea. I was forced to remember, and it taught me a lesson, that most committee members, and especially those on city boards, consider themselves as "budding" politicians and want the opportunity to express their opinions to the always large group of people in the audience. Reaching a consensus is not always easy.

I was a member of the South Florida Chapter of the Florida Planning & Zoning Association from 1959-1965, in which my dad played an important part, as former Director, Planning and Zoning, Miami, Florida. As President of the Association in 1959, he was an exceptional example of planning and conducting meetings. I feel I learned a lot from him.

Another experience—when we were active in a Baptist Church in Miami, where the Pastor had been a close friend of mine and my wife in high school days. The Pastor asked me to form a men's club or group for the purpose of broadening their interest in church and civic affairs. I did, and developed a fairly large group of men, where we held monthly meetings, with speakers invited from the civic community. I remember it as a challenge in "selling" the idea to the men of the church. I made every effort to respond to questions, ideas and opinions of the men and the program, overall, was successful and enjoyable. Putting a meeting together and making it enjoyable and worthwhile for participants requires all of the points I describe in managing a meeting.

One more example on meetings—also of a personal nature. When my wife and I retired and moved from New York to Port Orange, Fla we settled into a new neighborhood called "Deep Forest". On arrival, on the front door was a notice of zoning change for the surrounding area. Having had experience with zoning programs, I studied it, considered it to be a disadvantage to us and our neighborhood, obtained the proposed plans, posted them around my garage walls and invited all neighbors to take a look. They agreed with me and asked me to represent the neighborhood at upcoming city meetings, which I did on numerous occasions. This resulted in the neighbors asking me to form an association. I took on the task and after writing and rewriting a constitution and by laws, with help from a steering committee, called a meeting of all residents. This was the beginning of what turned out to be a series of regular meetings. The process we followed, realizing that even though not a "business meeting" in the sense of a company business, it took application of every one of the principles we describe.

Establish purpose for meeting—(this required input from others, our committee chairmen and city staffers). Purpose is most important item. In this example, it could be affect on property values, speeding on streets or crime prevention)

Determine number of participants—In our case, we of course included all Deep Forest residents and on occasion, city personnel involved in the topic. This was necessary to provide for parking, seating, food/drink, and handout material.

Determine location—(we used the Civic Center on the river front), Determine date—(required coordination with city)

Planning—providing for above and including support for speakers, like slides and sound.

Notified participants—published and distributed a flyer

Developed the agenda—invited speakers

Conducting—Invite questions and comments, using every courteous means but explaining to group, keep questions and comment to the subject.

Concluding and closing meetings.—Review decisions, conclusions, and follow up plans.
Period of socializing—coffee and snacks

Even though the above were not company business meetings, it seemed appropriate to include them as examples of the basics of meeting management and emphasizing the fact that conducting a meeting can be a pleasurable experience.

Note of possible interest: As a result of my frequent meetings with city staff and officials, and not intended, I was invited to become a member of the Port Orange Planning Commission, followed by a tour on the Port Orange City Council.

G. BUDGET PLANNING AND PREPARTION
It almost goes without saying, that to be a good and effective manager or leader, one has to have an understanding of the financial aspects of the organization or company.

Establishing a company or organizational budget requires a coordinated effort between corporate or departmental offices and each management area affected by and required to work within the constraints of the budget. It is important that the preparation of a budget be a shared responsibility of all management and that its purpose and application be clearly stated to all employees or members. The importance of management at any level being involved in the organization's budget planning cannot be over emphasized.

As an example, budget preparation at the ACTS Retirement Community begins at the corp. level, with an Exec. VP, Chief Financial Officer. The fact that ACTS is a non-profit organization is a major factor in its planning. Monitoring performance of and input from each of the 19 communities in six states is a major element in the preparation of the budget. In the effort of operating within the limits of a budget, maintaining good communication with all who are affected by the financial restraints of the budget is extremely important.

At PAA, we included budget planning in our management development program because it was felt that it was a very important part, of the communication process between all levels of management. Meetings of supervisory personnel were held to explain the process, request initial steps to be taken, provide budget data from earlier periods for review (feedback), and request steps to be taken.

While serving on the City Council, in Port Orange, Fla, a city of about 40,000 people, I had the interesting and educational experience of working with the City Manager, Council members, and departmental Directors, in helping to develop and implement a city budget. It took lots of input from each department head, drafting an overall budget, an awareness of revenue income, and a lot of communications with the city residents at several public meetings. Open, honest, and free two-way communication is always the key to success in budget preparation. It is important in business as well as civic affairs.

H. DELEGATION

Another BASIC management skill needed to be learned and practiced is how to delegate with confidence.

It is common knowledge that one person "cannot do it all". In order to be an effective manager at any level one must learn and practice good delegation.

All levels of management have to delegate—President of US, a company CEO, a PTA President, all levels of management. In the military it is called "chain of command".

A first thing is to "know your people". I.e., be knowledgeable of the educational background, cultural background, work experience and skill level, especially the degree of training in the work to be managed and then demonstrate confidence in the knowledge that a subordinate can do his/her job well.

It is important to build a level of confidence in the people you manage and make a practice of not interfering in the normal operation of the work being performed by another manager. If higher management bypasses a subordinate and communicates instructions to a lower level manager or employees, or a manager receives conflicting instructions from two higher level managers, it damages the ability of a manager to be effective. It puts a manager in the position of uncertainty as to whose instructions to respond too.

Example—true story from Bill Stearns—"My life as the manager of the sporting good department for a large department store was made "miserable by the fact that my three, or four, superiors never agreed on any thing. The Store Manager would insist that I display tennis clothing n' merchandise on the front aisle—later, the Group Manager would stroll by and insist that I display Golf clothing & merchandise. Then, bout that time, a Vice President would be touring the departments and insist that swimwear and vacation clothing be displayed up front! (Needless to say: my dept was always in a flux!) And the worry 'bout not obeying one, or the other, made me a nervous wreck."

Make a point of supporting people you manage in a manner of confidentiality that enables a subordinate to maintain an effective image and confidence with the people he/she manages.

Here's another example from Bill—"much as people love and respect our Pastor, there are some who get angry with him-'cause he tries to "control" every facet of everything the church does. (They feel he over extends himself-stretches himself too thin-and is far too reluctant to delegate!) Yet, if you were to ask Pastor, he'd hardly admit that he is possessive bout his leadership! So, even while he may be a "controller", I don't think you'd find that "feedback" threatens his position; he's open to feedback!"

When asked how she selected board members to support her, a past PTA President (my wife Marguerite) said "I just selected people recognized for being "good" people i.e., people known to be smart and for good and fair judgment".

I. PERSONAL DYNAMICS

At PAA, this was a very effective purchased program and workshop for developing the human, personal aspect of being a successful manager or leader. To learn about this program, I attended one of the seminars for several days, in Minneapolis, MN. Fellow attendees represented companies from around the US and other countries. I considered it to be an unusually well planned and beneficial program. I recommended it to our management and received approval to include it in our in-house program.

This was a 3-day seminar, held at several off JFK airport hotels, attended by approximately 48-60 men and women from most departments, including foreign stations. It provided for an instructional guide, loose-leaf binders and paper material on a wide variety of subjects. Arranged at 6 persons to a table, it was a stop watch timed program, with appropriate material distributed for each project, so that, starting with an empty binder, at the end of the 3 days, each had a binder full of discussed and learned material. Most all projects depended on a team approach to solutions. Thus, this offered an opportunity for a demonstration of natural leadership.

In my recollection, this program provided such a wide range of subject material that each "student" might benefit from different items. The course helped the participants learn, in meetings, the importance of time limitations, to read written material quickly, to draw conclusions, to develop a plan or make suggestions, and to realize that in many cases input from others can be of benefit in reaching conclusions. Finding solutions was the goal. An important feature related to the problems which come from judgment or misjudgment prior to knowing the facts.

Conducting this series was challenging for me because it involved so many of the elements taught in our training program—planning, logistics, timing, meeting management, communication, etc.

I appreciated the fact that my wife could assist me by distributing material to tables while I described and timed each project. Arranging for the provision of coffee-pastry at a critical time for a "break" was important to the program for it allowed for the informal discussion and mixing of participants. Meeting fellow employees from other levels of management and other departments provided for much of the learning experience.

At later times, it was always good to hear from participants of the benefits they received from this program. I consider this type program to be one of the better methods of management development/supervisory training and I recommend it.

J. TRAINING

It was always recognized as an important responsibility of and benefit for Pan Am management to provide the means and opportunity for employee training in all areas of the organization. One must realize that employee's technical skills are greatly dependent upon supervisory skills. Management at all levels must be aware of the skill level of subordinates and work to provide mentoring, training, guidance, and support where there is a recognized need.

Pan American was always recognized for its high level of TECHNICAL AND SAFETY PROCEDURES training.

Training of mechanics in all skills was an on going program and of real value in the times where it was beneficial or necessary to reassign mechanics from one specialty to another. For example, during periods when it became necessary to "layoff" mechanic personnel, it became possible for a person to request a reassignment to another specialty where he was also qualified.

Whenever a new item of equipment or a new model aircraft arrived it resulted in a great deal of specialized training. I remember at the time when the B727 aircraft was planned to arrive, a car pool companion was an instructor in the training department. In the car pool we listened to the latest of technical information daily. (I had had an interesting visit to the Boeing factory and walked thru the fuselage of a B727 under construction)

There was one time when the Chinese had bought some B747s. A large group of their mechanics were sent to the Boeing factory for familiarization and then brought to Pan Am for technical training. As I observed the young men in classes, it seemed strange to see a group of young "communists" being instructed by "capitalists". It was an evidence of how Pan Am management was respected in the airline industry and the world.

The pilot training at PAA was notable throughout its life, even to the extent of a flight training academy on 36th st, Miami. Used by many outside groups.

The point to be made, in summary, is that each member of management has a distinct responsibility to assist those he/she is responsible for, to grow in knowledge and capabilities and encourage creativity.

SUPERVISORY TRAINING.-

A fellow resident of the ACTS retirement community, Ralph Scott, a retired Division Manager, AT & T phone company, offered the following items from his experience with management training. These are excerpts from his material.

One of the most difficult problems of management is getting agreement on the standards of performance used to measure the effectiveness of final product, the accuracy of the item produced, the marketability of the product and how employees present the company's name. All of which affect the business profitability.

Agreement—In order to establish standards of any task it is important to gather together the affected management, top down and to decide on the standards expected for a product or performance. This process involves group dynamics. Agreements should be organized and set down in writing.

Evaluation—as standards are completed, start the evaluation of a process, marketing approach or performance of employees. In manufacturing, standards established should be used to measure accuracy, timing, work habits and expected production. With outside sales, the supervisor will use the standards to measure a sales person's knowledge of the product, sales knowledge and techniques, adaption of the product to the customers need and his ability to account for his activity.

Methods of training—Using the appropriate technique for training is very important if the supervisor or manager wishes to make changes.

Some of the techniques involve group discussion, visual aids, roll playing, case studies and practical application. The methods of goal setting, evaluation and training is applicable for management employees as well as line employees. Higher managers should do concerted observations of subordinates managers according too the standards of the higher managers agreed upon standards.

Result—In order to be successful with any plan of management, it takes the support of the owner, CEO or partners. The principal has to address the concept; otherwise the lower management team will not accept the methodology.

This is always a weakness in the management business getting the right set of standards of producing and performance.

Another Peter Drucker quote, "Plans are only good intentions unless they immediately degenerate into hard work."

General Colin Powell is well recognized for his leadership skills, both in military as well as civilian circles. An internet search of "Colin Powell-leadership" provides several sites outlining his thoughts dealing with techniques for personal improvement in leadership and, even though he is dealing with the military, many of the points aptly apply to business management as well.

His "A Leadership Primer," uses 18 lessons and I note only the topic of each of his lessons, and suggest readers refer to the internet search for a full description of the topic.

1. "Being responsible sometimes means making some people angry". (edited);
2. "The day soldiers stop bringing you their problems is the day you have stopped leading them. They have either lost confidence that you can help them or concluded that you do not care. Either case is a failure of leadership";
3. Don't be buffaloed by experts and elites. Experts often possess more data than judgment. Elites can become so inbred that they produce hemophiliacs who bleed to death as soon as they are nicked by the real world."
4. "Don't be afraid to challenge the pros, even in their own backyard."
5. "Never neglect details. When everyone's mind is dulled or distracted the leader must be doubly vigilant"
6. You don't know what you can get away with until you try."
7. "Keep looking below surface appearances. Don't shrink from doing so (just) because you might not like what you find."
8. "Organization doesn't really accomplish anything. Plans don't accomplish anything, either. Theories of management don't much matter. Endeavors succeed or fail because of the people involved. Only by attracting the best people will you accomplish great deeds."
9. "Organization charts and fancy titles count for next to nothing."
10. "Never let your ego get so close to your position that when your position goes, your go goes with it."
11. "Fit no stereotypes. Don't chase the latest management fads. The situation dictates which approach best accomplishes the team's mission."
12. "Perpetual optimism is a force multiplier."

13. "Powell's Rules for Picking People:" Look for intelligence and judgment, and most critically, a capacity to anticipate, to see around corners. Also look for loyalty, integrity, a high energy drive, a balanced ego, and the drive to get things done.
14. "Great leaders are almost always great simplifiers, who can cut through argument, debate and doubt, to offer a solution everybody can understand."
15. "Part 1: "Use the formula P=40 to 70, in which P stands for the probability of success and the numbers indicate the percentage of information acquired." Part 2: "Once the information is in the 40 to 70 range, go with your gut."
16. "The commander in the field is always right and the rear echelon is wrong, unless proved otherwise."
17. "Have fun in your command. Don't always run at a breakneck pace. Take leave when you've earned it. Spend time with your families. Corollary: Surround yourself with people who take their work seriously, but not themselves, those who work hard and play hard."
18. "Command is lonely".
Leadership is the art of accomplishing more than the science of management says is possible."

K. PERFORMANCE EVALUATION

The management performance evaluation process is a means of communicating between each level of management on an individuals work performance and is closely related to and an important tool in determining training and developmental needs.

It serves several purposes—

It provides the individual with an understanding of his/her superiors' perception of his/her skills, abilities, and accomplishments.

It provides a means of expressing complimentary comment of above average quality of performance and workmanship.

It aids in determination of salary levels, (In some companies, performance is related to salary bonus)

Performance improvement needs recognition. It serves as evidence of good communication and as a means of assisting an individual in awareness of his/her shortcomings and recommendations for developmental training.

The evaluation process is usually managed by an appropriate form, initiated by management in each position for each subordinate position. An important item on each form is the recognized manner and method in which each person evaluates his/her subordinate.

Even though the process is managed by a form, it is always recommended, that an evaluation be completed by a "one on one" personal meeting. It is always helpful for a superior to explain some of the written evaluations and allow for a full understanding.

L. Managers Responsibility for adding new employee

One of the important requirements of the management position is the responsibility for adding a new employee to the crew or staff. In a large organization of course, this function is mostly accomplished by a personnel department. In some instances however, when a specific background is required, a manager of a department is called upon to interview a prospective employee and make the decision to add a person to the staff. I had that experience when managing a group of systems Analysts in New York.

I found this element of supervision challenging and interesting. Applicants for computer systems design were from a varied background and represented even different cultures. I had the pleasure of working with men and women from India, Argentina, Taiwan, Estonia, as well s from different locations in the United States. Sometimes language became an interesting part of the work accomplishment.

For example, in those days, after completing a feasibility study to justify the need for a computer system, systems were designed by the Systems Analyst as a flow chart of instructions for coding by a programmer. One analyst from Taiwan spoke such broken English; I usually accompanied him to our Computer Systems Department in the Pan Am Building in New York City to help communicate with people to do the programming. He was very knowledgeable in the design of aircraft reliability programs and did an excellent job but needed help in communicating.

A manager doing the hiring assumes considerable responsibility for the performance of the new employee and must help with educating and training where necessary. When called upon to make the decision to add an employee, a manager must be knowledgeable of company policies and procedures. The person interviewed must leave with a good impression of the company, whether hired or not.

CHAPTER 8

PROJECT MANAGEMENT
"Project management is where leadership comes in"

Let's define "project" as a goal with specific intended results—to take a complex problem and disaggregate it into more manageable components with well-defined scope and interfaces with other components as well as external interfaces then organize staff to match the Work Breakdown Structure (WBS)

Many projects originate with ideas and suggestions from employees within an organization. Large projects, when accepted by upper level management, are assigned to those where a determination is made as to area of need, purpose, and feasibility. Areas of responsibility are delegated and goals and time tables are established with expected results

The process for the manager is to define tasks, assign tasks, require accountability, monitor performance and make adjustments, to keep focus on result.

In reality "changes" are the norm—requirements always change and change management is focus of much management activity, i.e. tradeoff benefits vs. cost.

Projects may vary in size and scope and naturally depend upon the type of work involved. On large projects, I enjoyed being a part of a "team". If I wasn't the lead, I liked working with someone who I respected as a leader.

While managing the group of Systems Analysts in New York, one of the interesting aspects of the work for me was responding to requests from Maintenance Dept Directors for a computer program which they felt they needed. These were considered "small" projects requested by departmental Directors, like Engine Overhaul, Aircraft Maintenance, Component Overhaul shops, or Ground Equipment Maintenance for what they would consider a need for information. Remember, at that time we were using punch card computer systems and output paper reports. Punch card data collection devices were installed throughout the shops, primarily for material control.

The Analyst assigned the project would first develop a "feasibility report" to estimate the cost, and a determination if the information could be provided by possibly a manual system rather than a computer system. It was always difficult to respond by advising that a manual system would work as well. A proposed computer system would be defined in flow chart format.

Since large projects are established by management at an upper level and usually involve more than one department, coordination and communication are the most important factors. Most large projects I was involved in can be considered "coordinated projects".

When assigned a project, which would be recognized as an element of a "coordinated project", the first thing to do was to" define and obtain agreement of goal of project and review the status of resources". (for example—who is needed to assist, what equipment and materials were needed, what tools were required, what programs needed, locations involved, to whom to report status, anticipated cost and savings, projected time period and preliminary target date)

Many reading this book will possibly have been involved in more complex and major projects than I, however, I will briefly describe projects from my experience—which I feel represent the elements we have suggested are important in project management i.e., establishing purpose, setting goals, planning, defining tasks, implementation, and monitoring performance. I emphasize—Communication with all parties involved was always most important.

I must stress the fact that projects are always a "team" effort and, to reach the goal, it takes a leader and a great deal of cooperation on the part of all concerned.

Constructing the Jet Center at JFK airport in New York, I remember as being a pretty major company project for Pan American Airways. Planning and coordinating the move of the Miami group to the new base, to join New York personnel, and functions, involved many people.

Some background of one project I was involved with concerned identification and control of aircraft components. At an early period at Pan Am, a committee, primarily of Engineers, but including cooperation between the manufactures and other airlines, developed a program of identifying those items to be classified as "components". The determination, of course included the elements of importance, reparability and cost.

A major means of control was the assignment of a code number to each component, and there became a "component code book". Control methods included a frequently modified tag. It was a famous yellow (buff) three part tag, A-B-C. One part would primarily provide record of its overhauled status; when installed, a part would provide info with reference to installation; when removed from service, a tag part would provide info with reference to date, removed from, reason, location, and other pertinent info of help to the overhaul shop.

This component tag was a major source of information and data for Maintenance in manpower planning; Production Control, in clerical staffing and records management; Purchasing/Supply in material support; Engineering in diagnostic studies/engineering changes; and Reliability in developing statistical data. Development of various control systems followed, based on this basic method of collecting information,

In Control Procedures, we developed administrative procedures for the flow of the tag stubs and information to be applied to them, or taken from them, by each group. Then when I was Manager/Systems/Procedures I was involved in a project to establish/improve accountability of aircraft components. It was clearly a goal which was recognized to be an evolving/developmental goal and so no time or date was possible. The project started in Miami but was extended to New York because components were moved between the two bases.

It was determined that a part of a method to maintain a control would be in the form of a data collection system to provide information. (I referred to this item in the area of my personal move to New York.).

My part in the project was the

a. determination of type equipment (IBM)
b. planning of physical shop /hangar locations and installation requirements (elec wiring, etc) and providing a current status of the expansion thru shops.
c. Since we were working with IBM punch cards at that time, we worked closely with the Data Processing Dept
d. Establishing a method of having a punched card flow with a component/part and be entered at each stage of its flow.
e. Design and develop computer programs to provide management with decision making / beneficial data.
f. During the process it was important that we maintain good communication with union leaders and all employees, and work with their cooperation.

Note: At one point, in New York, it was determined that the IBM equipment was not meeting our requirements, so after an evaluation study, we switched to Data Pathing Incorp. (DPI)

The project went through many stages and variations in development but, overall was considered by management as a successful program. Computer systems and informational reports continued to e developed as ongoing projects from this method as well as from the basic computer tag.

Another project of our Systems/Procedures group was similar to the Component control program. Its purpose was to identify and establish control over the class of aircraft items called repairable parts. It was recognized that many parts removed and replaced were repaired when the value was questionable. Some were discarded as not considered worthy of time and effort to repair. We felt this area was worthy of examination as an economic consideration.

I was given approval to form a committee to examine all aspects of the repairable parts process. I called it the Repairable Parts Analysis Committee (Repac). The committee represented Maintenance, Production Control, Engineering, Purchasing/Supply, and Budget/Cost Control, representing both Miami and New York.

A group of parts was selected and evaluated, with unit cost, repair cost, and maintenance needs as some of the factors considered. Frequent working meetings were held with groups as large as 20 members sometimes. We reviewed the data and made recommendations based on them with many instances of costs savings. I prepared minutes and, in addition to members, distributed them to heads of all departments concerned, as project status reports.

The meetings required all the elements outlined in the Meeting Management section, and although another project with a "movable goal", received full cooperation, was appreciated by Management and considered a successful program.

Another project which I was always proud of at PAA and experienced a small part of, was the efficiency of its aircraft service and overhaul maintenance preparation. It took in all elements of project management. Even though all airlines follow similar programs to some extent, this was accomplished at Pan Am thru a coordinated team effort between Maintenance, Operations, Engineering, Reliability, Supply, Systems/Procedures, and Data Processing. This was normally a routine scheduled event so that when an aircraft arrived all required elements were in place and the work proceeded smoothly. Flight log book items had been analyzed for non-routine requirements and included with the scheduled items. Maintenance supervisors were provided with data guiding them with work assignments of all categories—hydraulic, electrical, metal, and mechanical, etc, and material was prepared and provided for efficient handling. Teamwork, with good leadership, was the key to success for this regularly scheduled project.

Another example, of a personal nature, while on the City Council of Port Orange, Fla, the Mayor assigned me the "project" of having a city golf course constructed. He assigned me, probably because I had been on the Planning Commission when we developed the first City Comprehensive plan and it included a golf course. It turned out to be a project in the true sense of the word. It involved—with steering committee support, a feasibility study, setting a goal with a vision, organizing, planning, and communicating. It turned out to be a championship course called "Cypress Head".

In summarizing, planning and managing a project, although challenging, is an interesting element of a management position and responsibility and an opportunity to practice leadership.

CHAPTER 9

PROBLEMS WITHIN MANAGEMENT REFLECTING
LESS THAN LEADERSHIP QUALITIES

My approach to the subject of management has been to consider men and women who represent qualities of leadership in a positive manner.

However, to be realistic, unfortunately, in human nature there are too many examples of weaknesses in people who have reached leadership positions but failed to produce results necessary to a healthy organization or society. Many problems within an organization are the result of poor communication.

Lee Iacocca, formerly the recognized leader of the Chrysler Corporation, has recently (2009) written a book with a topic "Where Have All the Leaders Gone? In this book he is strongly critical, in a general way, of the many business and political "leaders" who have failed to show initiative in times where a true leader is needed to come forward with creative and constructive ideas and to recognize problems and develop solutions. I am quoting one line which represents the essence of my book "These are times that cry out for leadership".

There are companies, undergoing considerable financial stress in recent times, who show a "frustration" in their management decisions which reflects on lower management with uncertainties in project planning and of individual's personal security. These are times when management must use sincere communication and trust in support and accept advice from all employees. A manager, at any level, who feels that higher level management, is not as effective as they could be, should refrain from criticism, and instead, develop and submit constructive ideas.

The positive thoughts I have offered are

(1) The goal of good management is to maintain a positive attitude of team relationship with employees, with a high level of morale. As previously stated, comfortable communication is a key element in reaching this goal. Sometimes this area is a shortcoming.

(2) Management at the higher levels, when establishing policies, procedures and schedules, must make every effort to keep in mind the effect they have on the personal lives of subordinate personnel.

The most difficult thing—A person trying to be a good manager finds unreasonable demands a business places upon his/her personal life, sometimes by a specific higher manager. Some companies believe that they are your ONLY priority.

Sometimes a manager is so devoted to "being a good manager" that priorities are overlooked with reference to his/her personal life, and or not understood or appreciated by the organizations management policy. It behooves each individual to establish personal priorities and find a way to balance and maintain good working relationship with his organization.

Unfortunately, in recent times there have been too many examples of recognized "leaders" in industry and the work place that have forgotten and failed to follow the basic principles of a leadership position. There have been many reports of large company leaders who have ignored the trust employees and the public had placed in them. Their actions and decisions have reflected a lack of integrity, the lack of recognition for simple human relations, and a failure to accept responsibility for the affect their decisions have on the lives of others.

However, in our observations, we want to hold to our recollections of the many exceptional, thoughtful, and considerate leaders we have known and read about over the years. We want to encourage readers to search out, pay attention to, and follow advice from those determined to be "good leaders".

CHAPTER 10

CONCLUSIONS

In drawing conclusions, it behooves us to finish with an "upbeat" attitude, to avoid remembering negative experiences, and to concentrate on the positive aspects of being a manager-leader in the present and future.

In reviewing some of this material, Ray Valeika made a suggestion which gave me much thought. He suggested that "maybe your recollections should arrive at a common theme of what are the elements of your definition of success".

After some deep thinking, and attempting to further summarize my experiences, the words that came to mind, and I would consider a "theme", are "earned trust". Webster's definition of trust is" firm belief or confidence in the honesty, integrity, reliability, justice, etc of another person or thing".

I believe those whom I consider to have been a success in management, as a leader, were considered trustworthy and sincere in relations to others and held high moral purpose in his or her judgment. They led by inspiring others through example, encouragement and constructive advice. I believe a person can be a good leader in management if he or she has earned the trust of those whom they lead and communicates clearly the expectations of others and what others should expect of the leader.

In further thought, in reviewing my career, I mentally divided it into periods which I considered of "most interest". I think, in everyone's career, there are periods where the environment is more "exciting" than other periods. So, in reviewing this thought, I wondered why. I thought of periods where the subject was new to me, required a lot of thought, study, exploration of new knowledge, and enjoyable. Those were periods where there were clear challenging opportunities, and I could anticipate and help produce satisfying results. Those were periods where my manager supported me and allowed me to be creative and to develop ideas for improvement in our area of responsibility. So, in addition to "earned trust", I believe a good manager, to be a leader, must make an effort to recognize capabilities of a subordinate and align projects that will serve as challenging opportunities. It follows then, that each member of the management team, at any level, must make an individual effort to be creative, imaginative, and search out opportunities to make the "environment" exciting.

With reference to training and development programs, Management development programs should be a budgeted item and expenses controlled accordingly. Training is results oriented, and management should be informed of progress and results. Best results are obtained when higher management participates in the program.

Employees who do well and those who demonstrate leadership qualities should be recognized and supported accordingly, like scholarship programs, financial aid, etc.

As stated earlier, management skills can be taught, learned, and practiced, but true leadership, which has been described and examples offered, comes primarily from within as a natural desire to serve others.

It is my belief however, that if a person becomes aware of, and conscious of, a lack of those qualities, he or she can, by self examination and desire, improve personal relationships with others and develop these leadership qualities.

Recognition of a need for change can result from a church sermon, a good book, a class, an article in the newspaper, an appeal from a friend, a subordinate, or others.

I retired from Pan Am August 31, 1980, from the position of Manager, Management Development/Supervisory Training, and although I had not reached an "upper level" position in the company, I had been allowed to manage a group of fine men and women in a variety of activities considered key elements in the operation of the airline.

I always enjoyed and took pride in the work we did. I enjoyed the privilege and responsibilities of management, and interaction with the group. I was always shown courtesy and encouragement in personal contact with members of higher management.

Following a wonderful "send off" at a fine restaurant on Long Island, sponsored by colleagues, Marguerite and I returned to Florida. I feel honored to have worked with such a high caliber and skilled group of men and women, in all departments, who made Pan Am the great company it was.

I feel thankful for the support and opportunities I was allowed at Pan Am and have good memories of the exceptional leaders who served the company over those years. It is regrettable that Pan Am was unable to continue operations, in large part and generally, to world conditions but the loss of the airplane over Scotland was probably the "last straw".

It might be well to summarize a major theme I hope I have communicated through this book. To become a leader, one must have earned the trust of followers and have a desire to lead by serving others. A leader must be able to establish a goal, determine the steps necessary to reach a goal, develop a self motivational character to study, learn from those with experience, and emulate those whose leadership they respect.

Though I have used my experience with Pan Am for most references, I consider the subject of leadership in a broader sense. I consider the term a major item of concern in all aspects of our lives. The word "leader" is so often used in today's news, whether it be business, governmental affairs, sports, politics, or otherwise, I am more certain than ever that the search for leadership is a major concern for people in all walks of life.

It is my hope that, with the thoughts expressed in this book, someone may become more aware of a need to change or improve, and benefit in some way.

We sincerely wish our readers GOOD LUCK in the effort to be better leaders in management.

ADDENDUM

John M. Stearns

Bachelor, Business Administration degree, major Aviation Management, Univ of Miami, Fla,

Over 42 years with Pan American World Airways, (30 years in Miami and 12 in New York) supervised and managed groups of staff personnel in special fields, incl, engine scheduling and control, maintenance administration, Industrial Engineering, Control Procedures, Systems and Procedures, computer systems design, and as Manager, Management Development/Supervisory Training, conducted a series of management development/supervisory training programs.

Received a "Certificate of Recognition" for presentation at Latin American Division- Miami, Fla, Maintenance Program.

Received Performance Merit Award, Pan Am Maintenance & Engineering, for management educational program.

Outside of Pan Am, served on City Planning Commissions in Miami, Fla and Port Orange, Fla and City Council, Port Orange, Fla

Formed and served as first president of homeowner's association, 275 home subdivision, in Port Orange, Fla